Carnival of Lamps

Words for Prayer and Reflection

Cliff Reed

2-4-30

The Lindsey Press
London

Published by the Lindsey Press
on behalf of The General Assembly of Unitarian and
Free Christian Churches
Essex Hall, 1–6 Essex Street, London WC2R 3HY, UK

© Clifford Reed 2015

ISBN 978-0-85319-086-8

Designed and typeset by Garth Stewart

Printed and bound in the United Kingdom by
Lightning Source, Milton Keynes

I have brought my light...
to join the carnival of lamps.

(Rabindranath Tagore, 'Gitanjali')

The Poets light but Lamps –
Themselves – go out –

(Emily Dickinson)

This book is dedicated to the Unitarian congregations of
Ipswich and Framlingham in Suffolk, England, whom I served for
thirty-six years, from 1976 to 2012, and who appointed me their
Minister Emeritus in 2013.

CONTENTS

PREFACE

Quite where poetry ends and prayer begins I am not quite sure – at least as far as I am concerned! Prayer does not have to be poetry, of course, and some would say, with some justification, that the purest prayer is that which is uttered *in extremis*, with no thought as to its form, poetical or otherwise. It is, quite simply, a desperate reaching out to God – nothing more and nothing less. And certainly, not all poetry can be said to be prayer, even if the best comes from some nearby niche in the psyche. There is, though, a long – very long – tradition of marrying the poetic with the devotional. The Hebrew Psalms, and their translations in the King James Bible, are examples of this, as are sections of the Book of Common Prayer. This tradition recognises that when prayer is considered, the quality of its form and language enhances its power to open the heart and elevate the spirit. In my experience, the writing and the reading of poetry can involve the spiritual in a way that prose rarely does, except in the work of exceptional writers. Prayer itself comes in a number of forms, among which is the contemplative. From this tradition comes what we often call 'meditations' or 'words for reflection'. In this latest collection, then, there are prayers, poems, meditations, and words for reflection – plus a couple of hymns. I offer it for use in gathered congregations, in small groups, or for private and devotional reading.

Cliff Reed
Ipswich, Suffolk

February 2014

FOR PRAYER AND REFLECTION

*'And now nothing remains but to lay our offering on
the Altar of God...and to let his blessing rest on it and on those who
turn to it for help.'*

(James Martineau, *Common Prayer for Christian Worship*, 1862)

BY MANY DIFFERENT PATHS

O God,
the Ultimate, the One,
we, who came here by many different paths,
greet you and bow before you.

We were not just placed here on this planet.
We grew with it, out of it,
yet always in its web of life.

We were many things before we were human.
We were many humans before we were
'thinking man', as we like to call ourselves.

We are the children of more ancestors
than we can imagine, carrying the genes
of many things we cannot name.

We are part of this earth, this cosmos,
and we pause in wonder at its majesty.

Somewhere, some time,
creatures came out of all this that could
love and be kind, and recognise in you
the source of love and kindness.

Who were the first we don't know,
and never can, but we would be like them.

May it be so.

PARTAKERS OF THE DIVINE

'...whereby are given unto us exceeding great and precious
promises: that by these ye might be partakers of the divine nature.'
(II Peter I: 4)

We are products and partakers of the Divine,
whether we like it or not,
as are all things that live, all things that exist.

With our minds we explore the mystery that is Divine,
seeking light in darkness
and darkness in light.

As our souls seek communion with each other
in love and fellowship,
so they seek and find the Divine.

We cannot see God face to face,
yet we encounter God all the time and everywhere,
if we have eyes to see and ears to hear,
senses to connect with what is around us –
and spirits to reflect.

The Divine is the Great Mystery
we can never really know, and yet
the Divine is no mystery at all.

May we have the clarity and the humility
to realise it.

ASPECTS OF GOD

God of our inmost selves
and of the stars from which we came;

who is both the core of our being
and the transcendent mystery;

of whom there is no need of proof,
because we are here to ask the question;

to whom all true religion points, but whom no religion
can ever truly comprehend;

who is the truth behind the sacred myths,
but whose whole truth no myth can capture, however sacred;

who inspires the words of prophets and poets,
but who cannot be defined in words alone;

whose presence we sense where there is love,
but which we lose where there is hatred;

God of our hearts,
we turn to you in the communion of silence...

God of the silence –
in ourselves, in this sacred place,
and in the cosmic void,
bless us in our quietness and our tumult,
in our striving and our rest.

Amen.

FAMILIES

God of our hearts, we give thanks for all that is good and
loving in the families of the world:

> their care for each other;
> their forgiveness of one another's follies and offences;
> their tender welcome of the newly born;
> the care and guidance they give their children;
> their understanding and forbearance
> with the headstrong ways of youth.

We give thanks for the commitment and responsibility of
adulthood; the gentleness and kindness of parents, which hold
firm in all trials, making of the family a place of safety and
security.

We give thanks for the respect that is given to the wisdom and
experience of maturity, and for the compassion embracing the
frailty that may one day overtake us all.

We give thanks for those who have passed from us, to take
their place with the ancestors who gave us our roots. We hold
them in fond memory.

God of our hearts, we give thanks for our own families and all
they give us.
May every family on earth be blessed.

Amen.

BRITAIN'S DREAMTIME

'The stillness of the dead world's winter dawn
amazed him, and he groan'd, "The King is gone".'
(Alfred, Lord Tennyson, 'Idylls of the King')

'...there is written on his tomb this verse: "Hic jacet Arthurus Rex,
quondam Rexque futurus".'
(Sir Thomas Malory, 'Le Morte d'Arthur')

When Arthur ruled in Camelot
there was peace and joy in Albion.

His knights fought for the weak,
and truth and right prevailed.

They quested for the holiest,
and the purest found it –

when Arthur once was king
in Albion's pleasant land.

But now he sleeps in Avalon,
our once and future king.

When Arthur wakes
and rules again in Camelot,

there will be peace and joy
in Albion once more –

a future dream to match the dream
of a past we wish was true.

BEAUTIFUL PEOPLE

We have all seen the beautiful people,
with their perfect skin,
their features sublimely balanced,
their bodies so exquisitely proportioned;
moving with their mesmerising grace,
filling the air with their sweet voices.

And we give thanks for them.
We give thanks for the beauty which they bear,
as we give thanks for all the beauty with which
the earth is graced. Let's not begrudge it them.

But the beauty of their fragile bodies,
like the beauty of a flower, cannot last.
One day, sooner or later, it will fade.
One day, they will join the rest of us.

But there is a beauty that can last our whole lives long,
the beauty of simple kindness,
the beauty of a loving spirit,
the beauty of holiness.

For that we pray,
be we beautiful or not!

THE WORD

*'In the beginning was the Word, and the Word was with God, and
the Word was God.'*
(John's Gospel, 1: 1)

God is the Word
for the beginning
for what began the beginning
for what was at the beginning
and what has been beginning ever since.

God is the Word
for what is
and why it is
and how it is.

All words are in the one Word,
all words are in the one breath,
all breaths are in the one breath
that has breathed since the beginning.

And the first breath
was the first word at the beginning,
as our first breath was our first word
at our beginning,
and the Word was God.

THE BOOK OF BOOKS

'...of making many books there is no end.'
(Ecclesiastes 12: 12)

The Book of books, some call it,
and so it is,
not because it belongs on a pedestal
but because there's nothing quite like it:

a book of stories, myths, and legends;
a book of poems, hymns, and lamentations;
a book of ruthless politics and sacred history.

There is something there to express every feeling,
to match every mood, to suit every occasion.

There is love and passion there, fear and elation.
There is victory's triumph and defeat's despair.
There is cruelty and compassion,
slavery and liberation.

There are tales of loyalty and tales of betrayal,
the highest ideals and the basest villainies.
There are words of wisdom and power,
words of comfort and words of bitter loss.

There is exultation and wonder at the glories of creation.
There is the prospect of desolation and promise of restoration.
There is depression and madness, and righteous anger at the
world's injustice.

(continued overleaf)

There is the strife of nations and of empires,
the feuding of tribes and families,
the inner conflict of the soul in torment.
There are faith and doubt, credulity and scepticism,
humility and overweening pride.

We read of natural, everyday lives, and we are swept into wild,
psychedelic hallucinations.
We read the words of bards and prophets, sages and list-makers.

There are kings and heroes, queens and heroines.
There are tax-collectors and prostitutes; lovers, fishermen,
soldiers, and law-givers.

There is a carpenter and a tent-maker.
And there are men who failed the greatest test,
and women who passed it.

Life and death, goodness and evil, war and peace,
sex and violence, joy and sorrow –
all are there, and all that we human beings do
and feel and hope.

There is no single theology, no one answer,
no one voice, no one vision, no single perception
of the mystery we call Divine.
No book deemed holy accommodates
so many contradictions, so many versions that cannot
all be true, so many circles that cannot be squared.

The Book of books is the words of men and women, inspired
and uninspired.
It is the word of humanity in all our shades and depths,
virtues and aberrations.
And that, perhaps, is what also makes it the Word of God,
echoing and whispering through the tunnels of the human soul.

. . . .

ADDENDUM – A NEW BOOK OF BOOKS?

If, like those ancient scholars, I had the task
of assembling scriptures, of compiling a new
Book of books to last for generations,
a collection of words timeless and eternal to show
that 'revelation is not sealed', where would I start?

And where could I possibly end?
Where could I stop and choose on the way from
Mother Julian to Mary Oliver, by way of Machiavelli,
Wordsworth, and Martin Luther King?

IT IS CHRISTIANITY TO DO GOOD

A recasting of words from 'The Life of Our Lord',
by Charles Dickens

Let us remember that
it is Christianity to do good always,
even to those who do evil to us.

Let us remember that
it is Christianity to love our neighbours as ourselves,
and to do to all as we would have them do to us.

Let us remember that
it is Christianity to be gentle, merciful, and forgiving,
and to keep those qualities quietly in our own hearts
and never boast about them.

May we show our love for God
by trying humbly to do right in everything.

And if we do this,
and remember the life and lessons of Jesus Christ,
we may hope confidently that our sins and mistakes
will be forgiven, and we will be able to live and die
in peace.

May it be so.

THE WOMEN

Salome and Susanna,
Joanna and Martha,
and all those Marys – the mystic,
the Mother, and the Magdalene,
the wife of Clopas,
the mother of the Sons of Thunder...

These were the women
who walked with Jesus,
who cared for him and comforted him
when the men drove him to distraction,

who were with him when he died,
and knew he could never die.

But they were turned into prostitutes or plaster saints,
they were forgotten or suppressed.

Today we remember them, and lift them up
as the real women that they were.

And we too will walk with Jesus
in humility and love.

May it be so.

THE LAST DAYS
A meditation on Mark 13: 5–8

Jesus said, *'Many will come claiming my name and saying,
"I am he".'*
May our hearts and minds beware all who dress their
arrogance, hatred, and ambition in the clothes of faith.

Jesus said, *'When you hear of wars and rumours of wars, do not be
alarmed. Such things are bound to happen.'*
There is no easy way to peace. May despair never overwhelm us
when fragile hopes fail.

Jesus said, *'For nation will go to war against nation, kingdom
against kingdom'*
In every age, that has been true. The Last Days are always with
us.

Jesus said, *'There will be earthquakes in many places; there will be
famines'*
Unthinking Nature combines with human folly, bringing
misery and death without justice or distinction.

Jesus said, *'These are the birth-pangs of the new age.'*
This age can be one of wisdom and compassion if we will make
it so, with firm resolve and prayers that give birth to actions.

The vision of a better world is true, whatever happens. May it
be bright in our lives, however long the world must wait.

DISCIPLES
'We knelt down on the beach and prayed…'
(Acts 21: 5)

O God,
who makes the sun to rise
in glory over the shining sea
and causes the waves to lap
eternally on the shore-line,
be with us as another day begins,
and help us to be true disciples of Jesus.

Whether our life's journey be across
billowing oceans or along hard roads,
help us in our resolve to make it
with love in our hearts
and compassion in our hands.

This we ask in the name of him we follow
and in the spirit of all his messengers,
apostles, and fellow-voyagers.

Amen.

Aldeburgh, Suffolk
24 November 2011

TRANSCENDENTAL THOUGHTS

When we look at the world, there is that within us which orders the world, not simply observing it; an intuitive sense that transcends and comprehends the multiplicity we experience.

When we look at a physical object – be it a table, a planet, or a human being – we see its dimensions, its shape, its material properties; but in doing so, we sense that there is a lot more to it than that!

When we explore the natural world, the human world, the infinite deeps of space, or the infinitesimal minutiae of quantum physics, we sense and know that we, the explorers, are one with the explored; that the fact of our existence is one with the fact of all existence.

When we talk of God, we talk of that which flows between our own being and all being, immanent in both, transcendent in both, connecting both.

APPROACHING DIVINITY
Based on words by William Ellery Channing (1780–1842)

Creator Spirit, within our hearts and moving among the stars, we approach you with the powers and capacities you give us.

We approach you whenever we invigorate the understanding by seeking truth; whenever we invigorate the conscience by following it, rather than our passions.

We approach you whenever we receive a blessing gratefully, bear a trial patiently, or encounter peril and scorn with courage; whenever we perform an unselfish deed, or lift up our hearts in true adoration.

We approach you whenever we resist the habits and desires that are in conflict with our higher principles; whenever we speak or act with moral urgency and devotion to duty.

So may your Divinity grow strong within us, and the religion we profess blend seamlessly with the life we lead.

Amen.

DIVINE UNITY
Based on John Goodwyn Barmby's prayer for Unity Sunday (1865)

Divine Unity,
in you may all perfections be combined
in a glory of goodness.

In your Oneness we rejoice,
as in the fount of all being
and the heart of existence.

To your one and undivided will
we submit our varied desires
and our discordant passions.

(continued overleaf)

Eternal One,
be over us and within us, and may we
glory in your kingdom, love your laws,
and strive to make your rule of justice universal.

Amen.

THE ONE AND ONLY GOD
Based on words by John Goodwyn Barmby (1820–81)

If we really love the one and only God with a clear perception
of the Divine Unity, then the warmth of our love will spark a
like feeling in others.

May this warmth, this holy fire, enflame our souls and so be
kindled in those around us.

May we so truly worship God that others will be led to worship
in the same spirit.

And so may the warming glow of faith spread all around us, as
the sun rises and fills the heavens with light and glory.

O God, in the awareness of our true unity and of your glorious
Oneness, we delight to surrender our wilful divisions; to see
the possibilities of your goodness and to rejoice in service,
praise, and worship.

Amen.

IN ONE DIRECTION

Our lives move in one direction, but we need not fear the destination. There are worse things than journey's end, if end it be...

Worse things, like living without purpose, living without love, living without ever having seen the gossamer in autumn.

Spirit of Life, we are grateful for the things we need for our existence – our food and drink, our shelter from the storm, the clothes on our backs; the basics that everyone on earth should have.

But, as Jesus said, 'life is more than food'. Help us to receive with gratitude the things we need to *live*: the loving touch, the word of comfort, the vision of earth's glory, the sense of your presence in all Creation.

Above all, help us to know you in ourselves and in those we meet – though sometimes we make it hard.

Our lives move in one direction, there is no going back. May joy be ours on the journey; joy in sharing it with those who share the Way. However long the road, however hard, help us, amid the tears, always to find reasons for laughter, song, and praise as we travel together.

May it be so.

DOES GOD REALLY CARE...

Does God really care what name or pronoun we use when we speak of the Divine?

Does God mind whether we stand or kneel or sit to pray? Or which way we face when we do?

Does God care whether we worship in silence or in song, with poetic beauty or in stumbling prose, so long as we do so in spirit and in truth?

Is God bothered about what we wear and how – or if – we cut our hair, so long as it's our own free choice?

Does God mind what we choose to eat from Creation's smorgasbord, so long as we do so with gratitude and with deep respect for the life we all share?

Does God have the slightest interest in our theologies, doctrines, and dogmas – or in the squabbles we have about them?

Did God really lock up the truth in a few old books, imprison the Spirit in dead words, and then speak no more?

Does God care a jot whether those who minister to us are black or gay, male or straight, white or female – so long as they do so with humble, loving hearts?

Is God really as mean, as petty, as narrow-minded, and as down-right stupid as we too often are in the sanctification of our own bigotry and prejudice?

Perhaps all God wants is for us to be kind to each other, to be fair and just in all our dealings, and to be responsible in our stewardship of this good earth, our common home.

May it be so!

HELL IS...
'...my flesh shall rest in hope, because thou wilt not leave my soul in hell.' (Acts 2: 26–27)

Hell is what happens
when love has died
in the human heart.

To be unloved is to feel the touch of hell.
To be unloving is to be in it.
To be unloving 'in God's name' is to be of it.

Grace us with Divine Love, we pray,
for against it the gates of hell shall not prevail.

I'M NOT RELIGIOUS, BUT...
'For the letter killeth, but the spirit giveth life.'
(II Corinthians 3: 6)

'I'm not religious,' he tells me, 'but I am spiritual' –
as if there was a difference,
though when you see what often passes
as religion, you can see why he says it.

(continued overleaf)

But just as religion without spirit is dead –
a construct of rules, harsh judgement, and inhumanity – so
'spirituality' without religion,
without the refining discipline of the shared search,
slips too easily into self-indulgence
and fruitless fantasy.

The spirit gives life and the letter may kill,
but religion at its best brings us together
in loving, testing, sharing community.
And spirituality is better shared.

BE AS FRIENDS
*'Believers, whether men or women, must act as friends to one
another...'*
(Qur'an 9: 71)

O God,
who is the fount of mercy and compassion,
the will for justice and liberty,
be with your daughters as they tear off
the veils of oppression and separation,
cast aside the false dogmas that are used
to deny their full humanity.

Be with your sons and teach them
that the way of violence and terror
is not the right path and leads only to hell,
whose mouthpieces its preachers are.

Help all People of the Book, all believers,
all people with love and goodness in their hearts,
to embrace as friends,
for humanity is One as you are One.

Amen.

THE EXPLORATION THAT AWAITS US
Based on words from 'All Good Things', an episode of 'Star Trek: The Next Generation'

What is the exploration that awaits us?

Is it mapping the stars or studying the nebulae?

It may include these things;
indeed, the human spirit demands it.

But there is more, and we can do it
where we are in space and time.

It is charting the unknown possibilities
of our own existence.

TODAY
'Take no thought for the morrow.'
(Matthew 6: 33)

We can't save the world yesterday,
because that's already gone.

We can't save the world tomorrow,
because that will never come.

But maybe, with God's kingdom in our hearts,
we can help to save the world today.

UNANSWERED PRAYER
'Prayer doesn't change things. Prayer changes people, and people
change things.'
(Unitarian Universalist wayside pulpit)

O God, who doesn't seem to answer prayer,
who leaves the hungry to starve, the poor to die,
the oppressed to suffer, and the wars to rage,
why don't you answer prayer, if you're there at all?

But maybe that's the wrong question.
Rather, why don't *we*, humanity, answer prayer?

Why do *we* leave the hungry to starve
when there is food enough to feed them
and the means to grow more?

Why do *we* leave the poor to die
when there are resources enough
to heal the sick, clothe the naked,
and shelter the houseless?

Why do *we* leave the oppressed to suffer
for want of liberation, and wars to rage,
when we could stop them if the will for peace
ruled our counsels?

O God who can only answer prayer
with human hands, human courage,
and human caring, stir us to the love
that feeds the hungry and heals the sick,
strikes down oppression, frees the slaves...

You are the will for peace with justice.
You are the love that reaches out to us
from others in *our* need.

God of our inmost hearts,
who calls us to seek you there,
may we find you and so become
your loving presence in this
suffering world.

May it be so.

LOCATING GOD

'The Incarnation is true, not of Christ exclusively, but of Man universally, and God everlastingly.'
(James Martineau, 1805–1900)

'God is everything. Whenever I open my eyes, I'm looking at God. Whenever I'm listening to something, I'm listening to God.'
(Pete Seeger, 1920–2014)

'We created man. We know the promptings of his soul and are closer to him than the vein of his neck.'
(The Qur'an 50: 16)

There is nowhere where God is not.
The Divine is wholly present everywhere
and in all things,
and all things subsist within the Divine Unity.

Look out at the infinity of stars, you will see God.
Look at the green growing things, you will see God.
Look at the rocks on the mountains,
the sands of the desert, the waters great and small,
you will see God.

Look back through the aeons to the Beginning
or forward to the End, if there is one,
and you will see God.
Look at the myriad creatures that live with us
on the Earth – walking, flying, creeping, swimming –
you will see God.
Look at a woman or a man, a child or a newborn babe, you will
see God.

Look at love and kindness, grief and suffering,
hope and despair, darkness and light, you will see God.
Look into your own heart, you will see God.
Listen to the promptings of your conscience,
your deepest wisdom, you will hear God.

You may not always recognise God,
because there are many false images that can get in the way.
You may not be able to use the word 'God',
because it has been debased and misused too often.
But God is there nonetheless,
closer than the vein in your neck.

SALVATION
'...what must I do to be saved?' (Acts 16: 30)

'The harvest is past, the summer ended, and we are not saved.'
(Jeremiah 8: 20)

What does it mean to be 'saved',
to be saved in soul and spirit?

Is it about holding the right beliefs,
observing the right rituals,
saying the right prayers,
venerating the right saints?

Is it booking a place in paradise?
Stepping, by grace, from off some
predestined moving walkway to hell?

(continued overleaf)

Or is it being true to the best you know,
regardless of the consequences?
Living in honesty and authenticity?
Being as kind, compassionate, and loving as we can –
even when we don't much feel like it?

Could it be that to be saved is to live
free from hatred, vengefulness, and resentment;
free from hypocrisy and self-righteousness;
free from selfishness, jealousy, and greed:
to 'take no thought for the morrow',
because God's Kingdom is here, now,
and we are called to enter it today,
as living souls in living bodies –
not free from mortality but free from its dread?

To be saved is to live abundantly,
following as best we can in the footsteps of the great souls,
blessed with the courage to take hard roads.

GATHERING

*'And all the congregation worshipped, and the singers sang
and the trumpeters sounded...'*

(II Chronicles 30: 28)

*In the congregations that I served as a minister – as in others
within the Unitarian, Free Christian, and Unitarian Universalist
tradition around the world – it is customary to begin worship
with 'lighting the chalice'. The chalice represents the worshipping
community – freely open to all who come in goodwill – while the
flame symbolises the life-giving Spirit of love, liberty, and truth
which we hope will bless our devotions.*

WE KINDLE FIRE

We kindle fire
as people like us
have kindled fire
for centuries
beyond count.

We kindle fire
as people not like us
kindled fire
in the darkness
of time.

We kindle fire
as people like us
or not like us
will probably kindle it
until the world's end.

The world was born in fire
and it will end in fire
but here, now,
we kindle fire –

to say that we are one with all
who, in reverence and goodwill,
kindle fire today,
who have ever kindled fire,
and whoever will.

UNTIL EARTH ANSWERS
Based on words from 'The Tabernacles of God',
by John Goodwyn Barmby (1820–81)

With joy we light our chalice of communion!
May the flame in one heart kindle the fire in another!
May its light be shed into all the dark places,
and may soul inspire soul until earth answers heaven.

A MORNING LIGHT

May ours be a morning light to guide the young;
a shining noonday sun to make our life's way plain;
and a fire, warm and welcoming,
when evening comes.

WE GATHER IN FREEDOM
Based on words by Thomas Jefferson (1743–1826)

We gather in freedom, believing not what we want,
but what evidence proposes to the mind and conscience.

We gather to affirm both our own faith
and the right of others to hold theirs without restraint or
coercion.

Confident that truth is great and will prevail if left to herself,
we gather to seek her by insight and reason.

THE SPIRIT IS AMONG US

We gather in a house of peace,
where violence of hand or tongue
are unwelcome strangers.
The Spirit is among us as we breathe and sing and pray,
speaking gentle, kind, and friendly words.
Within us and through us may Divine Love reach out,
cooling hearts in which resentment burns,
warming hearts made deathly cold by hatred,
reviving hearts grown lukewarm with unconcern.

MASQUERADE

In a world where, too often,
bigotry masquerades as faith,
and hatred masquerades as doing the will of God,
we kindle this flame of hope –
hope that, in our worship, and our fellowship,
we will witness to a better way.

CARNIVAL OF LAMPS
Based on words from 'Gitanjali', by Rabindranath Tagore
(1861–1941)

We each of us bring our light
to join the 'carnival of lamps'.
We come as individual souls to gather in community,
finding our purpose in connection, our freedom in the self's
surrender, and our oneness in diversity.

THIS FLAME IS FOR PEACE

This flame is for peace
and love
and the community of Earth.

We kindle it
to outshine the flames
of tumult, war, and terror.

May it be so!

SWEET COMPASSION
Based on words from 'Dombey and Son', by Charles Dickens
(1812–70)

We light this chalice
in honour of all the weary and heavy-laden;
of all the wretched, fallen, and neglected
of the earth.

And we light it
in honour of all who have had compassion
for every suffering and sorrow.

We light it
in hope and resolve
that we will be among them.

LIGHT AND COMFORT

As tongues of fire
came to faithful people long ago,
so may the Spirit be rekindled
within us and among us today,
bringing the light of wisdom
and of loving fellowship.

CALLING DOWN FIRE

*Based on words by the Revd. Samuel Bury in a sermon preached
at Ipswich, October 1700*

We call down fire
in love, not wrath.
May it be to us a symbol
of the Spirit that makes us one.

REKINDLING THE FLAME OF LOVE

Based on words by Pelagius

We are called to rekindle the flame of love in our hearts;
to understand the needs and feelings of others
by discerning the same needs and feelings in ourselves.

FORGING COMMUNITY

For millennia beyond count,
in winter's cold and night's darkness,
people have gathered around fire,
feeling its warmth, seeing by its light,
forging community with food and work
and songs and stories.

In all the faith traditions of our kind,
fire has its meaning. And so we gather
round this candle's flame, sharers all
in the human spirit that makes us one.

'LISTEN TO THE PEOPLE...'
For election time (I Samuel 8: 7)

'Listen to the people,' God told Samuel long ago.
'Listen to the people,' we tell our politicians today.

In a time of decision, we kindle this flame
to light our own way to honest demands,
wise choices, and concern for the common good.

GENERATIONS
*'Generations come and generations go, while the earth
endures for ever.'* (Ecclesiastes 1: 4)

In humility we kindle our flame of hope,
pledging our transient generation's loyalty
to the Spirit who gives us life.

THE UNIVERSAL FLAME
Based on words from 'The Transcendentalist', by Ralph Waldo Emerson (1803–1882)

The Divine within us reaches out
to the Divine around us,
and the fire that burns concealed
in the ark of the heart burns too
as the broader universal flame
which makes our spirits one.

OLYMPIC CHALICE-LIGHTING
I Corinthians 9: 24–26

We light our torch to say
that together we run
the race of faith –
faith that the human race
is not run in vain.

PROPHETS OF GOD

As the true prophets of God have always told us,
the Divine will is for mercy and compassion,
love and justice.
May we, and all true worshippers of the one true God,
never suppose that vengeance and cruelty,
hatred and murder, serve the Divine purpose.
In the spirit of human solidarity and oneness
we join in worship.

THE IMPERISHABLE FLAME

In kindling this perishable flame,
we invoke the imperishable flame
that was kindled at the beginning
to enlighten the human spirit.

KINDLER OF THE STARS

Kindler of the stars
and of the fire at Earth's heart,
be with us now as we kindle this flame,
symbol of our own flickering spirits
as they reach out to you and to each other
in reverence and love.

BLESSING AND DISMISSAL

'Watch ye, stand fast in the faith...be strong.
Let all your things be done in charity.'

(I Corinthians 16: 13–14)

WITH LOVE AND COMPASSION

With love and compassion
for each other and the world,
may we go from here
more worthy of the gift of life
and of the blessings of the Earth,
our common home.

Amen.

OUR RELIGION
*A recasting of words from Charles Dickens' tribute to the Revd.
Edward Tagart (1844)*

May our religion have sympathy
for people of every creed
and venture to pass judgement on none.
May the lessons of Divine Truth
sink into our hearts and not be forgotten
in our practice.

AN OLYMPIC DISMISSAL

May victory be ours,
not in competition with each other,
but in the struggle with our own wilful selves.
May love triumph and its humble crown be ours.

IN THE SPIRIT OF JOHN BIDDLE (1615–62)

In the name of the One most high God,
Creator of Heaven and Earth;
in the name of his Son,
chief among his many sons and daughters,
our Brother, Jesus Christ,
who has no other than a human nature;
in the name of that Minister of God and of Christ
that is the Holy Spirit;
we go forth in the greater love that makes us one,
and in memory of all who gave their lives
for the truth that makes us free.

Amen.

INHERITANCE
Based on words from the Book of Thomas the Contender, a 3rd-century Gnostic Christian text

May the sun and the moon,
the air and the spirit,
the earth and the waters,
be fragrant to you.

May the sun shine on you,
that you may flourish with the grapevine
and so inherit the land.

OPEN THE DOORS
With thanks to the Revd. John Fairfax (1623–1700)

As we leave through the doors
of this Meeting House,
may we not forget to keep open
the doors of our hearts,
to welcome kindly the Spirit of God
and of loving human fellowship.

FOR ALL THE PROPHETS

For all the prophets through whom
God has taught us how to live
on this green earth, we give thanks.
May we heed their wisdom and be blessed.

CONNECTION

In the words, music, and quiet of worship
we have found connection with each other,
with the Source of Hope at our own being's core,
and with the Great Mystery whence all being flows.

We leave this sacred place with an inner light
to bless and guide us through the coming night
and through all the shadows that darken the days
of our lives. Go in peace.

FOR A FLOWER COMMUNION
Based on words by the Revd. Norbert Fabian Capek (1870–1942)

We ask a blessing as we part.
May we go from here to kindle hope
where sorrow's darkness reigns,
telling of those who overcame it
by the power of the Spirit.

In smelling the sweet fragrance of faith's flowers,
in breathing the air of compassion,
and in opening our hearts to those who suffer,
may our souls shine radiant as the sun.

May the warmth of Divine Love
flow through us to all our neighbours
on this good earth.

VESSELS OF YOUR LIGHT
With thanks to Michael Servetus (1511–53)

One and Undivided God,
who is the Creative Word,
the compassion of Christ,
and the Spirit that leads us into all truth,
bless us as we go out to be the vessels of your light.

WHAT THIS EARTH COULD BE

May we know in our hearts the paradise
this Earth could be,
and with the blessing of God
and in the footsteps of Jesus,
let us go out to make it so.

A WEDDING BLESSING
With words from 'Paradise Lost', Book IX

May God's blessing
be on................and...............
in their life together;
on the children they
have or may have,
and on us all.
In the words of John Milton,
'Be strong, live happy, and love.'

HEAVEN AND EARTH

'The poetry of earth is ceasing never.'

(John Keats, 1795–1821)

'Woof of the sun, ethereal gauze
Woven of Nature's richest stuffs...'

(Henry David Thoreau, 1817–1862)

THIS MIRACLE-PLANET

From Creation's light
we kindle our own light,
giving thanks for all the life
of this miracle-planet,
the life we are privileged to share.

FROM THE STARS

From the stars we have come:
of stardust we are made,
and to stardust we will return,
but for now we will walk
by the light of the sun
and worship by the light
of our holy flame.

FOR EVOLUTION

We gather in thanksgiving for the Earth
and the life-forms that have evolved
upon it and share it with us.

We bow our heads in sorrow
and kindle a flame in remembrance
for all those life-forms that evolved upon it
but which, because of us, are no more.

BEAUTIFUL DIVERSITY

May our flame of worship be to us
as the burning bush in which God speaks.

May it remind us of the Breath of God
that fills us and all the myriad creatures.

May we see its reflection in the water of life
that flows through Paradise.

May it bear witness to the beautiful diversity
to which this sacred Earth gives rise.

VOLCANO

Volcanic dust
can clear the skies,
restore celestial peace.
It doesn't last, but maybe, if it did,
could we learn to travel slowly once again?

To sail the seas in stately ships,
take trains across wide continents?
To walk once more the ancient ways
of trade and pilgrimage?
To see, to feel, the Earth on which we live –
and love her?

BIG BANG

If there was a 'big bang' –
and most scientists seem to think there was –
an infinitesimal moment in less than nothingness
when, suddenly, the show was on the road,
    creation *ex nihilo*,
then in that exploding point
between non-time and time
all the potential for what happened later was there –
    galaxies, neutrons, and dung-beetles;
    solar winds, *War and Peace*, fish'n'chips;
    love, Jesus, you and me;
    goodness, badness, and everything else
    that was, and is, and is to come.

There is not *a* God,
in whom to believe or disbelieve,
there is just God;
whatever it is that spans
all this space, all this time,
and laughs in a child.

OUR LOCAL STAR
' 'Tis first He steps upon the Vane –
And then – upon the Hill –
And then abroad the World He go
To do His Golden Will.'
(Emily Dickinson)

Down the millennia and all around the world
we have wondered at the sun, our own local star.

We have bowed in worship
before its awesome power.
We have named it as divine,
a god or the province of a god:

    bright Apollo and sky-riding Helios of the Hellenes;
    in Egypt, long ago, almighty Re –
    and the Aten of the heretic king;
    Frey, bringer of summer and good harvests to
    the cold northlands;
    to the Incas, in their doomed empire, Viracocha,
    who walked away over the ocean,
    promising to return some day...
    fearsome Huitzilopochtli of the Aztecs,
    thirsty for blood;
    benign Nzambi of Africa's Bacongo,
    the marvel of marvels and bringer of justice...

    Sun-gods all, consigned now to myth and metaphor
    – or to oblivion.

We say we do not worship
where reason and science have explained, and yet...
...and yet we wonder still.

THANKSGIVING FOR RAIN AFTER DROUGHT
'Rain is a blessing in our country.'
(Palestinian bus driver)

Thank you for the rain,
a blessing in a country
that has been dry too long.

Thank you for the rain,
bringing relief to parched fields
and giving hope for the harvest.

Thank you for the rain,
bringing soft green days
and a second spring.

Thank you for the rain,
healing cracked and dusty earth,
quenching its thirst.

Thank you for the rain.
We are sorry that we don't
appreciate it as we should.

IN A TIME OF FLOOD

'...the flood arose, the stream beat vehemently upon that house and could not shake it: for it was founded upon a rock.'
(Luke 6: 48)

'Why Bliss so scantily disburse –
Why Paradise defer –
Why Floods be served to Us in Bowls –
I speculate no more –'
(Emily Dickinson)

God of the Earth,
if you were the sort of deity
who sends the floods to punish us,
then we would beg you to recall the rainclouds
and spare us from them.

But you are not that sort of deity.
You are the God who has given us
the ability to tend the earth more wisely,
if we will, so that floods happen less often
and are less destructive when they do.
But we must choose wisdom over folly;
far-sighted knowledge over short-sighted greed
and wilful ignorance.

You are the God within,
who gives us the courage to endure the floods,
the love to help their victims and be with them
in their distress.

May it be so.

HOPING AGAINST HOPE
'Together...we have fought the long defeat.'
(J.R.R. Tolkien, *The Lord of the Rings*)

Since childhood I have loved the natural world,
been enchanted by its beauty
and intrigued by its ruthlessness,
aware of our baleful impact on the rest of Creation.

I have sorrowed at the devastated forests,
the species driven into oblivion,
the disappearing countryside and wild places.

I have heard much whistling in the dark,
even seen small victories,
but they are not enough.

Humanity is not a good steward
of this miracle-planet
and shows few signs of getting better.

So, I have never been an optimist.
But I do believe, as that peculiar phrase has it,
in 'hoping against hope':

hoping that we *can* do something
to avert the catastrophe
we have unleashed;

hoping that, beyond this Ragnarok,
something will be left in the tree of life
to come out and start again.

Let us never forsake the struggle,
let us hold our nerve and, hoping against hope,
keep faith with each other and the Earth.

After all, that pessimism could be misplaced.

May it be so!

GOD IS...

God is not so much a being
as the word we use when confronted
with the totality of all being,
the unimaginable ultimacy of the universe,
and the mystery of love
at work in the human heart.

MINERS

'Men master the darkness; to the farthest recesses they seek ore in gloom and deep darkness.'
(The Book of Job 28: 3)

When I was young
    there were mines nearby,
and miners on the buses,
    going to work, going home
with skins scoured white and
    eyes black-rimmed.

(continued overleaf)

Theirs was a world of darkness
    and of light, of danger,
comradeship, and harder work
    than I have ever done.

They were strong – as the
    crushing handshake of
one old miner always reminded me,
    along with his friendship and his faith.

Those mines are closed now,
    their way of life is gone,
their communities have crumbled,
    and we are the poorer for it.

When I hear of miners entombed alive,
    wherever they may be,
I think of those old mines, those miners,
    that old miner I once knew.

And I think of that strength,
    the strength all miners share,
and the faith that carries them
    through to deliverance.

I give thanks,
    God of the earth's deep places,
God of the light
    that can never go out.

STONES OF FIRE

'Thou hast been in Eden, the garden of God; every precious
stone was thy covering, the topaz and the diamond; the onyx,
the sapphire, the emerald – and gold... Thou hast walked up and
down in the midst of the stones of fire.' (Ezekiel 28: 13–14)

'Of Mines, I little know – myself –
But just the names, of Gems, –
The colors of the Commonest –
And scarce of diadems –'
(Emily Dickinson)

From deep-hewn mines they come,
won from the darkness with toil and blood and sacrifice.

Cut and polished with skill and craft,
they become the marks of wealth and power,
or tokens of gratitude and love.

As jewels, they sparkle and glitter on rings
and crowns and diadems;
maybe enhance the beauty of ankle, neck, or breast.

We cannot eat them when we're hungry,
but we can glory in their colours,
their enhancement of the light.

For this we give thanks, but save us from
the covetousness and vanity they can kindle.

Let our hearts be uplifted by the beauty,
but not corrupted by the brightness,
of these stones of fire.

TYGER, TYGER
Based on words from William Blake's 'The Tyger'

'Tyger Tyger, burning bright,
In the forests of the night'...
But no longer in the forests of
Bali, or Java, or the Caucasus.

'Tyger Tyger, burning bright' ...
But no longer in the forests of
Turkey, or Iran, or China.

'Tyger Tyger, burning bright' ...
But not for long, perhaps, in the forests of
Russia, or Indochina, or Sumatra...or even India.

'Tyger Tyger, burning bright,
In the forests of the night' ...

But everywhere your forests are falling, and soon
you may burn bright in memory and poetry alone.
Maybe then we will mourn the passing
of your *'fearful symmetry'.*

Miserere.

TRAMPLING DOWN MIRACLES

'With the multitude of my chariots I am come up to the heights of the mountains, to the sides of Lebanon, and will cut down all the cedar trees thereof, and the choice fir trees thereof.'
(II Kings 19: 23)

Creative Source of all things, known by so many names, we who have named you come now in sorrow and repentance for what we have done to your Creation.

We pollute your skies and poison your waters. We take too many fish from your dying seas; destroy the reefs and swamps that nurture them.

We drain your wetlands, clear your forests, hunt your wild creatures towards extinction and remove their shrinking refuges, leaving them no room.

The land we need to feed us we exhaust or cover with asphalt, bricks, and concrete, unwilling to restrict our numbers to what the earth can bear.

Much that is beautiful and fertile still remains, but the writing is on the wall for us, we who trample down your miracles of creation.

In sorrow and repentance we ask for wisdom and humility, that we may yet leave a cleaner, happier, more fruitful earth for all who share it.

STEWARDS OF THE WEB

'...clumsy carts drawn by oxen, whose ancestors were worn to death, as their unhappy descendants are now, by the suffering and agony of this cruel work.'
(Charles Dickens, 'Pictures from Italy')

'For it is written in the law of Moses, thou shalt not muzzle the mouth of the ox that treadeth the corn. Doth God take care for oxen?'
(I Corinthians 9: 9)

We are stewards, in our brief time, of life's great web on this small planet; made so by the twists and turns of evolution.

We are not masters of the Earth. It is in believing so that we have wreaked such havoc. Teach us humility, Great Spirit, lest we perish.

We are part of the natural order and its interdependence. We cannot float above its struggles, insulate ourselves from its cycles of life and death: they are ours too.

As stewards, we are gardeners and foresters, herdsmen and tillers of the soil. And sometimes we must take the place of things that we destroy, like Nature's hunters, the predators which keep the biosphere in balance, though 'red in tooth and claw'; for 'there is a time to kill' as well as 'a time to heal'.

Teach us, Great Spirit, to do both with reverence and compassion. But there is never a time to be cruel or to wantonly despoil. And neither is there a time to feel guilt at being who we are.

We belong here. We have a right to be here. We are children
of the earth, with all its blood and beauty, all its sentience and
insouciance, all its suffering and pain.

Like all creatures who breathe your breath of life – the lion, the
wolf, the bear; the great whale, the scurrying ant – we are your
vessels, Great Spirit, members of this good creation.

We are involved in it. We cannot live untouched or not
touching. Save us from being its pillagers and poisoners,
inflictors of cruelty. And save us from the sentimentality that
morphs into intolerance and hatred.

So may our brief tenure of the earth leave it rich in kindness,
life, and beauty.

'EXTERMINATE!'
'And the ants will inherit the earth.' (Anon.)

'Exterminate!' the Daleks commanded. And we did.

We exterminated so many things
that once walked the earth or flew above it,
that swam in its rivers or roamed its oceans.

And we are still doing it.

How long will there still be elephants and rhinos,
lions and tigers, vultures and eagles?

(continued overleaf)

How long will our closest relatives,
orang-utans and gorillas,
bonobos and chimpanzees,
survive our depredations in their shrinking rain-forests?

How long will birds still sing their dawn chorus
in our gardens and our countryside? How long will there still
be verdant gardens and real countryside?

And human beings have exterminated each other too, denying
humanity to people not quite like themselves and, in doing so,
abdicated their own.

Maybe we will exterminate ourselves,
for we have created the means to do so.

Everything that lives becomes extinct in time,
that's the way of the Universe;
but we shouldn't make anything extinct before its time,
with consequences we cannot foresee.

We are not Daleks, those monsters of science-fiction,
and we needn't do what they say.
So let's treasure life's web, humanity's diversity,
and not exterminate them!

May it be so!

IN THE GREENHOUSE

Slowly, slowly it happened,
the atmosphere changed.
Not as you'd notice straight away,
but changed it has, changing it is.

The forests and sea-creatures of aeons long ago
were hacked out, pumped out,
and burned, burned, burned –
    in factories, mills, and locomotives;
    in ships and trucks and 'planes;
    in homes and cars...
and slowly, slowly the atmosphere changed.

The Earth is warmer now,
not as you'd notice straight away,
but it is warmer just the same.
And it will get warmer still,
beneath our greenhouse roof.

And the Earth is changing,
not as you'd notice straight away,
but it is changing just the same.

Deserts grow, inch by inch, forests die;
bread-baskets wither and turn to dust;
the ice retreats, the sea rises.
Not as you'd notice straight away it rises,
but coasts and islands tremble.

(continued overleaf)

The Earth is warming, changing:
not everywhere at once;
not always in the same way;
not as you may notice, where you are,
but it's happening all the same.

Some people don't believe it.
Some people don't want to believe it.
Some people don't want you to believe it,
but it's happening all the same.

Slowly, slowly it has happened.
Maybe there's not much we can do about it now,
but maybe there is something.

Miserere

ELEGY FOR GUNPOWDER JOE
For a young cat killed on the road

He came into our lives
exploding with boundless energy,
with joy and mischief and curiosity.

He graced our lives
with his beauty and affection,
with his playfulness and vibrant life.

So swiftly he grew,
so swiftly he moved,
so swiftly he flashed through our lives –
a blur of ginger on his way to who knows where...

Mother Earth receives his still body,
but air was for leaping through,
water his endless fascination;
fire was his warmth and the light in his eyes,
which is now gone.

A brief life of little consequence his may seem,
but he was our Gunpowder Joe, and we loved him.

FOR PUD
Elegy for a cat whose time had come

Gentle, playful,
watching in the window;
sleek beauty in black and white,
ready at the door to welcome us home;
quiet, affectionate ballet dancer,
silently sensitive to the presence of grace;
my companion in work and prayer,
whose many intrusions were always welcome –
with love, we say farewell now.
Find peace after pain,
rest in this garden that was yours, for a while,
rest in the earth, Mother of us all;
for your brief life and the gift of your trust,
we give thanks.

COMMUNITY

'Beloved, let us love one another: for love is of God; and everyone that loveth is born of God, and knoweth God... for God is love.'

(I John 4: 7–8)

BEING THERE

O God,
whose Spirit is among us
as comforter and friend,
be with us in this time of new resolve.

Remind us that, as someone has said,
'the first duty of a congregation is to congregate'.

It matters that we come here when we can,
not just for what we each may gain
but for what we each may contribute
by our presence and participation.

Remind us, in our heart of hearts,
that if we want our church to be there for us,
then we must be there for our church.

And remind us that, if we want its members
to be there for us in our need, then we must
be there for them in theirs.

In our strength, may we be strong
for those who feel their weakness.
In our weakness, may we be ready to take
the proffered hand, for through it we may
receive the strength that is divine.

FENCES

Based on a sermon by Revd. Samuel Bury, Ipswich, October 1700

Let us never
put fences round
our faith.

Let us never
call down fire on those
who differ from us.

Let our religion,
in its breadth,
be the common bond of all union.

And whatever differences
may be among us in smaller matters,
let us unite in love with all people of goodwill.

OUR RELIGION – A REFLECTION

Our religion welcomes diversity of thought and belief,
recognising that this is in tune with the diversity of human
nature and experience.

Our religion upholds the freedom of each of us to be true to
our own insights and conscience in matters of faith.

Our religion allows for the possibility that other people's beliefs
are valid, in whole or in part, and we extend constructive
tolerance to other faith traditions and communities.

(continued overleaf)

Our religion makes no claim to hold a monopoly on truth, and questions the right of anyone else to do so.

Our religion is more concerned to affirm what is positive in our own belief-system than to be negative about what others hold to be true.

Our religion is more concerned with discerning the spirit of a faith-tradition, including our own, than with focusing too narrowly on the letter of its creeds, ordinances, and scriptures.

Our religion offers welcoming and loving community to all who seek us out without conditions – save that they come in goodwill.

Our religion binds us together in a free association where we, its members, can explore and celebrate the things of the spirit, both individually and together.

Our religion provides worship which, at its best, stimulates, challenges, and comforts according to need; which respects the spiritual and intellectual integrity of each worshipper; and which recognises that reason, emotion, and the fostering of fellowship all have their part to play in the experience.

Our religion recognises that the Divine is made manifest in an infinity of ways and places, and we reflect this in the diverse nature of our life as a worshipping community.

Our religion affirms the full and equal humanity of all people, and it exists to serve human need, recognising that religion was made for people, not people for religion.

THE PURPOSE OF RELIGION

The purpose of religion is
    to create loving community;
    to foster relationships of mutual caring and respect;
    to nurture the human spirit;
    and to comfort, challenge, and inspire us,
    as the need arises.

The purpose of religion is
    to seek and to find a moral compass for the soul;
    to make responsible use of the mind's powers,
    to help us become good stewards of God's green earth,
    and to be humble explorers of the universe.

The purpose of religion is
    to celebrate life in its fullness;
    to follow in the footsteps of those who have taught and lived
    the better way for humankind;
    and to uphold the universal values that make for
    peace, justice, and happiness the world over.

The purpose of religion is
    to free itself from inhumanity, bigotry, and empty dogma;
    and to serve the cause of human welfare in a global
    commonwealth, with joy and compassion.

THE RELIGIOUS GENIUS
A meditation on some words by Albert Einstein

In every age the religious genius transcends convention's narrow bounds to reach a cosmic consciousness.

It is a consciousness that knows no dogma, no God conceived in our human image.

In every age it is among the 'heretics' that, so often, this consciousness has dawned; among those branded 'atheist' and 'infidel' that religion has reached its heights.

Too rarely were they called 'saint'. More rarely still were their words heeded.

Let us reflect in the silence...

Guiding Mystery, help us to heed the truth and to honour the truth-tellers. May we feel what they feel and know what they know, for the world's salvation.

So be it.

A FAIRER PARADISE
'For, though that seat of earthly bliss be failed,
A fairer paradise is founded now...'
(John Milton, 'Paradise Regained', IV: 612–613)

'One world this, for all its sorrow...'
(Vincent Brown Silliman, 1894–1979)

God of our hearts,
whose will is for oneness and unity
among your foolish and disputatious children,
we confess our weakness for the things that divide us.

We would renounce the evils of hatred, injustice, and war;
the bloody idolatries of racism, nationalism, and bad religion;
the prejudices of gender, caste, and sexuality:
help us to do so.

So may we build communities, countries,
and continents where to be human means more
than the false loyalties that corrupt the soul
and which lay waste the earth.

We are One, as you are One, in our infinite variety.
Help us to know it and to live accordingly.

GETTING ALONG

Why can't we all just get along, God?
You don't care a hoot about our conflicting creeds, dogmas,
and theologies,
so why do we argue and fight about them?
Why can't we just be a bit more loving to each other?
Is it really so hard?

Why can't we give each other a bit more respect?
Why can't we be kinder and more forgiving?
Why can't we all live by a few simple rules
about honesty, consideration for others, and treating them as
we'd like to be treated ourselves?

Why can't we accept that it's enough to be part of the one
human family,
regardless of the labels we stick on ourselves?
Why can't we live together peacefully on this beautiful earth
without wrecking it?
Why can't we be content to have enough, and only be
discontent when other people don't?

Why do we persist in judging other people
instead of paying attention to our own mistakes?
Why do we have to be rude, nasty, and violent to each other
when it's so much better – and easier – to be nice?

God, why can't we all just get along?
Show us the right path!

THE GOAL OF RELIGION
'...be ye kind one to another' (Ephesians 4: 32)

Some say that the goal of religion
is to be 'saved',
to book a place in heaven,
to secure bliss in paradise,
to be rewarded, not punished,
in this life or the next.

But this is not the goal of true religion.
The goal of true religion is to be kind.
There is a well of loving kindness in our hearts,
replenished endlessly by grace, if we will only
draw upon it, use its living waters, and be saved
from the temptation to be unkind.

May it be so.

THIS HOUSE OF PRAYER
For the re-dedication of a Meeting House after restoration

God of our hearts,
whose voice is heard in the sacred places
of all humanity and who whispers in the hearts
of all who are prepared to listen:

We ask your blessing on our worship
and on this house of prayer,
which we re-dedicate today.

(continued overleaf)

73

We give thanks for the skill and labour
of those who have worked to restore and renew
its fabric, and we ask your blessing on them.

We pledge ourselves to fill it with our faith and praise.

This is a modest tabernacle, O God,
but may it still be a house of prayer
for people of all nations,
and for all humble, faithful souls,
 no matter what their creed.

We ask this in the spirit of Jesus and all your messengers.

Amen.

PRAYER AT THE CLOSING OF A CHAPEL
Bedfield Unitarian Chapel, Suffolk, 16 May 2010

God of those who worshipped here before us;
God of *our* hearts – we who worship here today;
we come before you with sadness
and with thanksgiving.

Sadness, because no one will worship here again,
but with thanksgiving for the years
of faithful witness and loving service
with which our forbears made of this humble place
a temple of your free and loving Spirit.

For those who ministered here,
and for all those they ministered to,
we offer our recognition and gratitude.

They didn't labour in vain,
for they brought joy and blessing in their time,
and that will stand for all eternity.

In a time of silence may we call to mind the people
of this Chapel, who worked and worshipped here
and served their neighbours in this village...

And now we turn from the past
and pledge ourselves to emulate
the spirit of service that brought this Chapel into being.

We will not do so here,
but you are not bound by walls,
however hallowed, and nor are we.
The world awaits your servants, as it always has.
May we be among them.

Amen.

DWELLING IN POSSIBILITY
'I dwell in Possibility –
A fairer House than Prose –'
(Emily Dickinson)

It is the fool, the Psalmist writes, who
'hath said in his heart, There is no God',
and closed his mind to possibility.

Spare us from the arrogance of thinking
we know all there is to know about God,
all there is to know about everything.

Spare us from the dogmatic certainties
of atheism and fundamentalism,
all authoritarian ideologies,
both secular and religious.

May we be always open to possibility,
never insulating ourselves
within walls of closed-minded certainty;
never hedging in the Great Mystery
within which we dwell;
never mistaking the words we use
for the realities they conceal;
never confusing the prose of philosophy
with the poetry of faith.

Whatever we may believe,
whatever our minds may tell us is true,
there is always the possibility that we may be wrong.
And we would be fools to think otherwise.

UNITED

'Let all the people praise thee, O let the nations be glad and sing for joy.' (Psalm 67: 3–4)

'One love, one heart, let's get together and feel alright.'
(Bob Marley and The Wailers)

Keep us united,
Spirit of Oneness,
keep us united where we already are,
and make us united where we are not.

Keep this land of many peoples united,
as it became united, step by step,
through centuries of rivalry, war, and conflict.
Save us from all that would divide us
and return us to a dark past.

May the quest for unity keep the peace
of this continent, the peace that came after
centuries of war and slaughter, the peace
where freedom and democracy replace
the rule of tyrants and despots.

May our faltering steps towards unity
find a path through the traps and pitfalls
that beset the way – for there is no easy way.

May awareness of the unity of humankind
supplant the false divisions that infest our minds,
the divisions of race and nation,
politics and ideology, sect and religion.

(continued overleaf)

Spirit of Unity, teach us that our rich diversities
need not be threatened by realising
the truth of our oneness.
And teach us also not to make false gods
of those diversities, idols demanding blood.

The enemies of unity are injustice, oppression,
inhumanity, unkindness, delusions of difference...

We are the human race.
We are the Earth.
We are united.

May it be so!

COMMEMORATION
AND MEMORIAL

'Write this for a memorial in a book...'

(Exodus 17: 14)

STILL DREAMING...

Remembering the address of Revd Dr Martin Luther King Jr at the Lincoln Memorial, Washington DC, on 28 August 1963; and with excerpts from his eulogy for Revd James Reeb, delivered in Brown Chapel, Selma, Alabama, 15 March 1965

We remember today a speech that electrified the world with a dream of freedom and equality for all God's children.

We remember the speaker, in whom the ancient spirit of prophecy spoke again, to raise up the oppressed and to rebuke the oppressor.

We remember the challenge it presents to us all, for its vision still awaits fulfilment.

We remember, too, a minister from our own household of faith to whom, as to millions, that speech was an inspiration, and for whom, two years later, its challenge led to martyrdom in Selma, Alabama.

It was a martyrdom shared by many in that great struggle for Civil Rights and for humanity, and we honour them all.

And we remember what Martin Luther King said of him:
'... *in his death James Reeb says something to each of us, black and white alike – says that we must substitute courage for caution, says that we must be concerned not merely about who murdered him, but about the system, the way of life, the philosophy which produced the murder.'*

Martin called James '... *this fine servant of God'*, whose '*innocent blood'* may yet be a '*redemptive force'*.

Three years on, Martin Luther King too walked the martyr's path. May his blood and his words continue their own work of redemption.

As the years pass, we still hope, still dream, with Martin – with James – and with all that honourable company – that '*Out of the wombs of a frail world, new systems of justice and equality are being born.'*

We shall overcome.

May it be so.

JESSE OWENS – BERLIN 1936
'Read me the name of the Olympic victor...
where it is written in my mind,
for I owe him a sweet song...'
(Pindar, c. 518–438 BCE, 'Olympian Odes')

Born in Alabama,
an unnoticed black boy
in Jim Crow days.

But he could run,
Oh! how he could run!
And that *was* noticed.

(continued overleaf)

At High School
it was noticed,
then at Ohio State.

Three world records
in nineteen thirty-five,
and then Berlin.

One hundred metres, gold!
Two hundred metres, gold!
Long-jump, gold!
Four hundred metres relay, gold!

Four gold medals in one Olympic Games,
another record broken.
Broken too, the Nazis' racist myths.

But not his homeland's:
they took longer.
As did the recognition.

Another medal,
the Medal of Freedom,
in nineteen seventy-six –

Forty years on
from Jesse Owens'
triumph in Berlin!

GREAT WAR CENTENARY: A REFLECTION

To the memory of Frederick R. Stephens, Imperial Yeomanry
1900–1901; Army Service Corps / Labour Corps 1915–1918

'In pastures green? Not always; sometimes He
Who knoweth best, in kindness leadeth me
In weary ways, where heavy shadows be...'
(From a prayer that Frederick carried to war.)

At this centenary of the Great War, as it was known for
twenty short years, think of someone who connects you to it:
a grandparent or great-grandparent, some other ancestor or
relative, or maybe someone else whose story has burned itself
into your consciousness.

I think of my grandfather, already a Boer War veteran, who
wore his uniform with pride, as one old photo shows; the
uniform he never scorned, nor doubted, nor denied. Patriot,
soldier, Christian, with a prayer in his pocket and his heart;
walking into old age with military bearing, despite the horrors
he had seen, the poison-gas he had breathed.

Not every soldier became a poet.
Not every soldier who came back
was disillusioned with the cause
for which he fought. Honour them too:
that is what the memory of my grandpa
teaches me, as he marches straight-backed
and proud through my childhood recollections.

You may tell a different story,
but let's respect them all,
for we weren't there, and who are we to judge?

REMEMBERING BOZ: 1812–1870

We remember and give thanks today for the life and work of Charles Dickens: for his genius as a writer and his sublime use of the English language; for the wonderful stories he gave us, and the panoply of characters who inhabit them; for his denunciation of social wrongs, his puncturing of pomposity and hypocrisy.

We know he was a man as weak and flawed as the rest of us. We know he often fell short of the highest that he knew, as we do. We know that, like us, he sometimes hurt those who loved him most.

But we still give thanks: for the good he did, the right he upheld; the untold pleasure he has given and still gives, so long after his own lifetime.

We remember that he shared with us a liberal faith, believing that the quest for human good outweighs the demands of all narrowing and unloving dogma.

It is not for us to forgive his transgressions, but neither should we judge, lest we be judged ourselves.

In generosity of spirit, may we celebrate his achievements and pray that our own lives might bear such rich fruit as his.

AT THE GRAVE OF THOMAS CLARKSON
Playford Church, Suffolk, late March

On Thomas Clarkson's grave
a simple bunch of flowers lies,
bearing the simple message – 'Thank you'.

Thank you, Thomas, for your courage
and determination to rid the world of slavery,
and the trade it spawned.
Thank you for your unfailing discipleship
in the loving Way of Jesus.

And thank you, O God, for raising up
Thomas Clarkson as an instrument
of your justice and righteousness.
Thank you for his years of service,
this friend of slaves.

May I be as zealous in the cause of right.
And although I know he was not alone,
that many other folk played their part in the struggle, save me
from the ignoble temptation to set them against each other in
history's memory, or to demean the faith,
the devotion, and the contribution of any of them.

At the grave of Thomas Clarkson,
on this beautiful spring day,
so remote from the hell of the slave-ships
and the plantations, I too say 'thank you'.

Amen.

'TERRIBLE THINGS AND WONDERS IN THE DEEP': REMEMBERING THE *TITANIC*

'Thou hast showed us terrible things and wonders in the deep, and we bless and glorify thy name for thy mercy in saving us, when we were ready to perish.'

(James Martineau, *Common Prayer for Christian Worship*)

On this anniversary of a fateful north Atlantic night, when a great ship was torn open by a mountain of ice, and fifteen-hundred souls perished in the cold darkness, we think of all who 'go down to the sea in ships' and 'do business in great waters' [Psalm 107:23].

The sea is still a perilous realm beyond our control. Let us hold in our thoughts all seafarers, all travellers on the whale-road, whatever their business, who face the dangers of storm and tempest, iceberg and hidden rock, piracy and war.

And we are grateful for those who are saved when 'ready to perish', and for those who save them.

Let us remember to respect the sea always, even when it is our playground and we take to it for pleasure and recreation. The Titanic is not the only craft to have been lost because of negligence, and folly.

Sunk by the hubris of men as much as by the iceberg, her tragedy is a lesson we must not forget.

The sea gave us life in the aeons long ago; it gives us life still. Let us be grateful for the ocean's gifts, neither wasting nor destroying them, lest it rise against us – 'Thou hast showed us terrible things and wonders in the deep...'.

[Note: the Titanic was lost on the night of 14/15 April 1912.]

THANKSGIVING FOR THE SO-CALLED 'TRINITY ACT' OF 21 JULY 1813
'There is one God; and there is none other.'
(Mark 12:29)

'Let us be duly thankful to God, who has put it into the hearts of those who were in power to listen to the plea of humanity and justice, and so to repeal...the code of persecuting law.'
(Revd. Thomas Belsham, Essex Street Chapel, 25 July 1813)

Divine Unity, One God of our One World, in whom there is no division, no multiplicity, but in whom we may perceive many aspects according to our diverse needs, we give thanks for the day when Parliament removed the penalties for holding Unitarian beliefs.

We celebrate the liberty of conscience thus gained; the freedom to worship you without fear or dissimulation; the right to be true to our own understanding of your nature.

(continued overleaf)

We honour the memory of those who strove to achieve this freedom; those who suffered discrimination, persecution, and even death, so that we could affirm what Scripture and the universe proclaim: that you are One, and that this universal Oneness in which we live, and move, and have our being is Divine.

And although we celebrate the day that set our own faith on the road to gaining civil and religious liberty, we recognise too the rights of all people of goodwill to think, believe, and worship according to conscience and without fear. So may our troubled world recognise its oneness and find peace.

We ask this in the spirit of Jesus, our brother, and of all who have gone about doing good, as he did, and known you as guiding love.

Amen.

THE DIVINE PRESENCE
With thanks to John Fairfax, one of the 'ejected' of 1662

God has instituted worship,
altars are found everywhere.
Once, a desert tent of meeting
housed a wand'ring people's prayer.

The Divine Essential Presence,
knowing well the bounds of mind,
more in one place than another
seems to come to humankind:

temples, meeting houses, churches,
for God's worship set aside,
havens for the human spirit,
refuges from foolish pride.

Differences of thought and custom
fractured what is really one,
slammed shut doors that once were open –
so new ventures were begun!

Forbears, true to heart's conviction,
would not bow to Church and State;
heavy-hearted were excluded
from their cherished temple's gate.

So they sought out meaner places,
found the liberty they bring
there to worship with good conscience,
and God's solemn praises sing.

[To be sung to the hymn tune 'Cross of Jesus'.]

A LIBERAL RELIGIOUS MANIFESTO

We stand for truth over falsehood, reason over superstition,
toleration over bigotry.

We stand for science in gaining knowledge of nature and then
applying it in the service of humanity.

(continued overleaf)

We stand for human equality and unity over racism, sexism, and homophobia; over nation, caste, and sect.

We stand for societies, communities, and families which are caring, compassionate, and fair; which practise personal and social responsibility, and which honour the full and equal rights of women as well as of men.

We stand for the right to cultural and artistic self-expression, provided that it respects the legitimate rights and feelings of others in its turn.

We stand for this planet's interdependent web of life, and pledge to live creatively and humbly within it.

We stand for peaceful ways of resolving our disputes, while recognising that the innocent must be protected.

We stand for freedom *of* religion, freedom *in* religion, and freedom *from* religion; the right to be true to your own conscience and to leave or to change your religion.

We stand for a liberal, democratic, and secular society – the best available guarantee of civil and religious liberty for all. We honour those who have striven through the centuries to achieve it.

We say that kindness and goodwill are the supreme test of any religion's claim to truth, and the arbiter of anyone's claim to follow it.

May it be so.

AN OLYMPIC PRAYER
I Corinthians 9: 24–25

In honour of their ancient gods the Hellenes gathered, under
the peaceful aegis of the Olympic truce, seeking αρετη –
excellence and fulfilment – in athleticism and all else that
made for manhood. Through fifteen hundred years the ideal
slumbered as the grass grew over ruined Olympia.

Now, as athletes of every nation gather from around the world,
preparing to compete in the Olympic – and the Paralympic –
Games, with the prayers of many faiths on their lips and in
their hearts, we give thanks for their dedication, and for the
excitement and exultation which their quest for excellence will
bring.

And we give thanks in hope that honesty, fair play, and
sportsmanship will win out over all temptation to cheat,
whether for money or for vainglory; to gain the hollow 'victory'
rather than face the honourable defeat.

We reflect on the Games of the recent past, calling to mind
the men and women whose prowess stirred our emotions,
and whose joy we presumed to share. For them and for their
achievements we give thanks.

And we remember the Olympic triumphs that meant more
than just winning a race; that took apart the lies of evil tyranny
and inhuman ideology; that were a victory for truth and right
and the human spirit.

(continued overleaf)

With sorrow we recall the times when all semblance of Olympic truce was lost to war or shattered by terrorists. With these tragedies in mind, we pray that any who would break the truce this time will repent, or be foiled if they won't.

May all who run, or jump, or swim, or throw, or otherwise compete, gain that incorruptible crown which comes with the victory of the spirit. In that race we can all take part and, by the grace of God, win.

May it be so.

TROUBLED WORLD

'No light, but rather darkness visible
Served only to discover sights of woe,
Regions of sorrow, doleful shades, where peace
And rest can never dwell...'

(John Milton, 'Paradise Lost', Book I)

MORE IN ANGER...

'...whoso shall offend one of these little ones which believe in me, it were better for him that a millstone were hanged about his neck, and that he were drowned in the depths of the sea.'
(Matthew 18: 6)

God of our hearts, we come to you in anger and sorrow at the evil in the world, at situations – maybe known to us and touching us – where injustice masquerades as law, where the abuse of innocence masquerades as its guardianship, where violation of the deepest bonds masquerades as their protection: situations where arrogance masquerades as service, where slavery masquerades as relationship, where malice masquerades as love.

We share the fury of Jesus at those who make an idol of imperfect law, who impose burdens where they should bring relief, who cause the downfall of little ones, and for whom it would be better to have a millstone hung around their necks and be drowned in the depths of the sea.

We seek assurance that truth will prevail, that human suffering will be relieved, that beyond the present darkness there is light.

We ask strength and endurance
for those bearing unjust burdens.
We ask for courage in standing for the right.
We ask for grace that righteous anger
will not give way to hatred.
We ask for wisdom and clear sight
to follow always the path of righteousness.

This we ask in the spirit of Jesus
and of all your messengers.

TOO MANY PLACES...

'The blood that stains our altars and our shrines,
*   Our fires, our sacrifices, and our prayers*
The gods abominate. How should the birds
*   Give any other than ill-omened voices,*
Gorged with the dregs of blood that man has shed?'
(Sophocles, *Antigone*)

There have been too many places where the murder done takes
on a horror and an infamy that makes their names a by-word
for the evil that men do; such names as My Lai and Srebrenica,
Rwanda and Halabja... places where the innocents were
slaughtered by men sunk deep in evil.

We cannot understand them and we cannot forgive them. So
we leave them to a judgement that will endure eternally.

SYRIA

Syria is an ancient land of many faiths –
Sunni and Shi'a, Christian and Alawite,
Druze and Ismaili...
many gods, but only one God.

The gods that spur men to hatred
and to murder are false gods,
no matter what their sect.

Only the God whose will is for
love and peace and kindness,

in our hearts and in our world,
is true, no matter what our sect.

Let the true God's will be done,
in Syria and everywhere else.

May it be so.

SINCE THE TOWERS FELL
For the 11th of September

Years lengthen since the towers fell;
since four planes, hijacked
by malice and delusion,
took war to America and the world;
since three thousand martyrs died,
drawn from many faiths and ninety nations.
And still they die, as the years pass,
choked and poisoned by those clouds
of deadly dust.

We pause in sorrowful remembrance...

Those who slaughtered the innocent
in God's name await divine judgement
on *Yawm ad-Din* for their blasphemy.
Their crimes are beyond our forgiveness,
so we must look to our own lives, our own souls,
and see what needs correction there.

Miserere.

AMONG THE RUINS
Meditation on Isaiah 61: 4

'Ruins shall be rebuilt...'
The shattered glass and smoking ruins that had been home or
workplace, ignited by the raging flames of greed and malice.

'...and sites long desolate restored...'
The looted shops and burned-out buildings laid waste by crime
and violence and the evil of the mob.

'They shall repair the ruined cities...'
The cities ruined by false and selfish values, by malign
subcultures that undermine community and betray us all.

'...and restore what has long lain desolate.'
The desolation wrought by moral vacuum, the neglect and
corruption of young souls that withers humanity in the bud.

Who shall restore? Who will rebuild? Who will give meaning
to the sacrifice of those who died?

People united and envisioned. People empowered and
awakened. People who are moved by love and athirst for justice.
May we be with them. May we be among them.

'Ruins shall be rebuilt and sites long desolate restored; they shall
repair the ruined cities and restore what has long lain desolate.'

TOO MANY DATES

God of our hearts,
too many dates are etched on our memories
on which we remember acts of murder
and terror committed in the name of faith.

We pray not to make of them what our ancestors made of dates
like November the Fifth and the Twelfth of July,
enshrining prejudice, hatred, and division.

We pray that remembrance of horror
will not lead to bitterness and a vengeful spirit;
that those who suffered injury or grievous loss
will be healed and comforted.

We pray that those who would kill and maim
will realise the evil of their false path,
ask forgiveness and find the better way.

We pray not to be tempted into blaming
the innocent for the crimes of the guilty.
We pray for wisdom and the love of neighbour
that Jesus taught us

God of our hearts,
we cannot forget those dates,
but may they be to us reminders
of your call to love and stand firm
for true humanity.

Amen.

DAYS OF SLAVERY

Spirit of liberty, God of love,
we remember today, as best we can,
the days of slavery:
when liberty was snatched away
and love was trampled underfoot;
when untold cruelty reigned
on slave-ship and plantation;
when even people counted good
lost sight of what your goodness
demanded of them.

We would rather forget the evil that was done,
but we must remember.
Be with us in our remembrance
and our sorrow...

We are ashamed of slavery,
but proud of those who resisted it,
grateful for the brave souls
who overthrew it, in your name and humanity's.

And we are conscious that slavery
and unjust servitude are with us still,
in this twenty-first century.
We pray and we resolve that those
who practise it will be confounded,
that those who profit from it will be impoverished,
and that those who suffer it will be set free.
And may we play our part in their liberation.

(continued overleaf)

We ask this in the name and spirit of Jesus,
who died for the truth that sets us free.

Amen.

AT A TIME OF DISASTER

For the dead, peace.
For the bereaved, comfort.
For the survivors, hope and help.
For the helpers, of all faiths and nations,
strength and the willingness to stay the course.
May this be our prayer as we worship here today.

'Lighten our darkness, we beseech thee, O Lord':
darkness of despair in the face of untold horror;
darkness of the closed heart and closed hand;
darkness that only love, given and received,
can penetrate and dispel.

O God, the impulse to love
and compassion in human hearts,
in the face of suffering that we cannot truly comprehend,
of disaster that has taken so many lives,
and could yet take many more,
move us to generosity of spirit
for our neighbours and their shattered world.
So might we do what we can
to bring your love to bear upon them
in their great affliction.

Amen.

AFTER THE GREAT WAVE

In Japanese mythology, earthquakes are caused by a giant fish
who lies imprisoned under a gigantic stone beneath the sea. When
the fish moves, it sets off a 'harbour wave' – or tsunami.

Namazu, the Great Fish, stirs
and the earth quakes.
Tsunami, the Great Wave, races
to the shore.
Harbours are engulfed, and towns
and villages and farmlands.
The fragile, perilous works of humankind
are assailed and shaken.
Nature's power and human folly combine.
People are filled with fear.
They suffer ruin, devastation, death.
Human weakness is exposed. We feel
helpless in the face of so much suffering.

And yet we cannot allow ourselves
the luxury of despair.
We are here to say that in us
the universe cares for its children.
We are here to reach out in love,
uniting our spirits in an affirmation
of hope beyond apocalypse,
and to do what we can.
And so, with that intent,
we kindle our sacred flame.

THE END OF THE WORLD IS NIGH: MEDITATION ON GENESIS 18: 23–32
A news story once said that an asteroid would hit the earth on 31 January 2019...

Tomorrow the asteroid strikes,
and off we all go into oblivion,
like the dinosaurs before us –

the murderers and the warmongers,
the drug-dealers and the embezzlers,
the child-molesters and the muggers,
off we all go;

the rapists and the gangsters,
the liars and the hypocrites,
 the oppressors and the deceivers,
off we all go;

the polluters and the loggers,
the wanton destroyers and casual exterminators,
meddlers with genes and wreckers of life's web,
yes, off we all go, our pride laid low –
the inheritors who squandered our inheritance.

Or are there fifty innocent upon the earth?
Or forty, or thirty, or twenty?
Or even ten? On all the earth?

'For the sake of ten I shall not destroy it, says the Lord.'

STANDING ON THE SIDE OF LOVE
'He that is without sin among you, let him cast the first stone.'
(John 8: 7)

We stand on the side of love, as Jesus did.
We stand on the side of love,
as all God's messengers, all champions of humanity, do.

The love that knows no false boundaries,
the ones that prejudice, ignorance, and fear erect:
boundaries of nationality and ethnicity, creed and sect, gender
and lifestyle, sexuality and sexual orientation.

We stand on the side of love.
We stand against hatred, injustice, and violence.
We stand against the bigotry that beats and shoots
and stones, and thinks itself righteous in doing so.

We stand against ideologies and theologies
which dehumanise human beings for being 'different'.
We stand against governments and institutions –
be they secular or religious – which persecute love
and those who love because they love.

We stand on the side of love, as Jesus did.
Help us to do so.

Miserere.

THE CIRCLING YEAR

'We are children of the earth, whose years must soon be spent; and yet, O God, we have beheld thy glory.'

(A. Powell Davies, *The Language of the Heart*)

THIS YEAR OF JUBILEE
Leviticus 25: 9 ff. and 'A Child's History of England', by Charles Dickens

In this New Year, as it resounds
with celebration and thanksgiving,
we pray for all who rule –
be their realm a nation or a home.

Remind them – and each of us –
that it can be a year of Jubilee,
a year for justice and liberation,
lifting burdens and restoring hope.

May those called kings and queens
and commoners, all of us equal in our humanity,
love justice, freedom, truth, and knowledge.

Teach us to do our duty
as members of the human family;
and should we neglect that duty,
remind us of it – whatever our status
in this commonwealth of Earth.

We pray that the stories and the spirit
of all good brave souls will still inspire us,
and that we will do our best while life is in us.

And may the spirit of Jubilee be with us through this
and every year.

WINTER'S PATCHWORK
Fynn Valley, Suffolk – January

Snow-melt
jewels the grass,
green amidst
the white and brown
of winter's patchwork mantle.
In the south
the reborn sun blazes.
A Robin, with glowing breast,
watches from
his naked thicket.

WHITE ON WHITE
Fynn Valley, Suffolk – January

A cold, grey day
with snow lying,
snow falling.
White on white,
an Egret rising;
a Barn Owl hunting
without breaking
winter's silence.
Across a snow-bound field,
a Roe Deer bounding.

LENTEN PRAYER AT IKEN CHURCH
Saint Botolph (or Botwulf) founded a monastery at Icanho –
now Iken – in Suffolk in the seventh century. The present church,
dating mainly from the twelfth century and dedicated to him,
occupies the site.

Botwulf, from within the gates of Paradise,
do you ever look down on this holy place?
Do you recall those years of prayer and struggle,
here between the river and the sky?

You came here to witness to the gospel
and to pray for the world,
for the world needed the gospel then,
and it needed prayer.

And now, thirteen centuries on,
it needs the gospel more than ever,
and it needs your prayer.
May my prayer join with yours
across the gulf of time:

O God, send your love into the hearts
of foolish, sinful humanity, that we may be saved.

Amen.

SPRING EQUINOX

We light our chalice to greet the Spring
and to rejoice in life's renewal,
pledging ourselves to be good stewards
of this beautiful, blossoming earth.

STRENGTH IS IN THE SUN

Strength is in the Sun,
birdsong is in the woods,
blossom is in the hedgerows.
Life rises all around us –
and in us too, if we will let it.
We open our souls to the springtime,
and give thanks that we are alive to see it.

PERILS OF THE SEA

We light our chalice in joy at springtime resurrection;
in thanksgiving for new life,
new members of the human family;
and, today, in remembrance of lives
lost to the perils of the sea.

SEASON OF HOPE

Give thanks for Spring! Here again,
with its promise ever-new,
with its many-yellowed flowers,
its bright songbirds proclaiming
their presence to the world –
a world darkened, as ever, by human folly;
by war and suffering undeserved.
But still give thanks for Spring,
the season of hope.

THE PATH TO EASTER
A responsive Lenten meditation

We kindle our flame of fellowship.
May it be to us a symbol of springtime's
returning warmth and the Divine Light
that shines in every loving heart.

The Lenten Fast is with us.
We remember the wilderness days of Jesus:
his lonely struggle with the inner tempter,
with wild beasts for company
and angels attending to his needs.
We struggle too, in a cluttered wilderness of busy-ness,
possessed by our possessions.
We leave no room for wild beasts or angels.
We cannot see the starlit glory of the desert sky.
Holy One, help us to be still.
And may our minds and hearts respond.

Everywhere Spring is waiting to explode.
Snowdrops give way to daffodils,
leaf-buds strain to open.
The season of birdsong is finding its voice.
And may our minds and hearts respond.

The wilderness is not a place to stay,
we are not born for solitude.
Jesus wrestled there alone
and won his holy struggle with himself.
Then he left it, knowing his purpose.
May we too leave the wilderness with new resolve.

The interactions of fertile ground
with light and warmth and rain
produce the miracles of germination and of growth.
Our ancestors danced and sang
to celebrate the time. We too rejoice
that, out of winter's dearth,
the life and plenty of the Earth are born again.
For we are her children and her dust.

Lent leads us to another resurrection,
but first the path of pain and anguish,
the path of betrayal and desertion.
The self's surrender is witness
to the truth of love.
On the cross, Jesus knew nothing of Easter Day.
We remember those who share his cross today,
martyred for love and for humanity.
When the third day dawns and we rejoice
at the spirit's triumph, may we not forget
their myriad Calvaries.

In the name of all who have walked the Way of love and sorrow,
Amen.

LENTEN JOURNEY TO CALVARY

Mark 1: 12–13

O God, be with us as we set out through the wilderness on our Lenten journey to Calvary.

Grant us courage in the face of enmity, and the love to end it. Give strength to those who are oppressed by tyranny, poverty, and war. Comfort all who are persecuted for their faith, for what they believe, or just for being who they are. As you were with Daniel in the lions' den, be with all who are unjustly imprisoned and in peril of their lives.

And as you were with Jesus, 'among the wild beasts', be with us as we live among your most wonderful creatures. Show us how to leave them room in our crowded world, with tracts of wilderness for their home and our renewal.

Grant us the wisdom to be good stewards of the Earth, with peace and plenty for all people, and reverence for the web of life. Save us from being greedy consumers of your Creation; from the folly that lays waste what we cannot restore, blights what we cannot heal, and devastates where we cannot remedy.

May we walk gently in the footsteps of Jesus and all great souls, as true friends to all your children and to the earth, our common home.

Amen.

WHO WALKED WITH JESUS

O God, who walked with Jesus
in the beauty of Galilee
in spring;

who walked with him
on the hard road to Jerusalem
and on the way of tears to Calvary;

walk with us, we pray,
and don't forsake us.

Amen.

NAILS ON A CROSS: FOR GOOD FRIDAY

Nails on a cross, a spear;
an axe, a sword, a gun;
the instruments of torture;
napalm, cluster-bombs, and poison gas:

so we kill humanity;
so we kill God;
so we kill the Divine –
    not in those we murder,
    but in ourselves.

(continued overleaf)

Today, above all days,
we remember this,
and repent.
Help us all to do so
on this blighted earth.

Miserere.

JERUSALEM, JERUSALEM
Luke 19: 41–42

Jerusalem, Jerusalem,
if only you had known
the Way that leads to peace, to peace,
and peace the world had shown.

Jerusalem, Jerusalem,
where once the Temple stood,
where now a Dome of gleaming gold
marks where the Prophet trod.

Jerusalem, Jerusalem,
where David's line once ruled,
where still his people pray today
beneath their holy wall.

Jerusalem, Jerusalem,
where Jesus preached God's word;
where he was praised, betrayed, reviled,
and nailed on the rood.

Jerusalem, Jerusalem,
where Mary brought the news
that she had seen her risen Lord
amid the morning dew.

Jerusalem, Jerusalem,
if only you could know
the Way that leads to peace today
and God's true Spirit show.

Jerusalem, Jerusalem,
a city and a dream,
God, grant us all a healing hope
and peace, your crystal stream.

THE RISEN CHRIST

*'...it is not Jesus as historically known, but Jesus as spiritually
arisen within men and women who is significant for our time...'*
(Albert Schweitzer, *The Quest of the Historical Jesus*)

Jesus didn't want to be worshipped, he wanted to be listened to.

He called men and women to follow on the path he trod, not to
build shrines and idols wherever his feet fell.

Jesus didn't work miracles to prove he was divine; he did works
of love to show that we can do them too.

Jesus didn't say, look at me; he said look to God and help me
build the Kingdom in this world and in the human heart.

(continued overleaf)

Jesus didn't go to the cross to buy back souls with blood; he
went to the cross because the path of love sometimes leads that
way. And when it does, we must take it, as he did.

The risen Christ was neither corpse revivified nor spectral
counterfeit. He is the community where compassion dwells,
with justice, truth, and loving fellowship.

ERA OF THE BOBOLINK

'It was as if a Bobolink
   Sauntering this way
Carolled, paused, and carolled –
   Then bubbled slow away!'
(Emily Dickinson, c. 1859)

'This is the era of the bobolink,' wrote Thoreau –
one day in May amid the bursting apple blossom –
the bobolink – that Emily Dickinson so loved –
but not here – not this side of 'the pond'.

Here, it is the era of the nightingale –
whose song explodes – bubbling and rippling –
through spring nights and summer days.

Give thanks if you can hear them –
bobolink or nightingale –
for eras have a habit of coming to an end.

WHITSUNDAY COMMUNION
Acts 2: 1–4 & 10: 38; I Corinthians 12: 12–13, 27

Living Spirit, who moved among the disciples at Pentecost, filling them with power to preach and witness, making of their separateness one body, be in us and among us now. May we, in our diversity, know a deeper unity and be the limbs and organs of the risen Christ that is humanity renewed. So may we reach out to do good, to heal, and to bring relief to the oppressed, as Jesus did. *Amen.*

[The Lord's Prayer may now be said.]

On the night of his betrayal, as so many times before, Jesus shared a meal with his companions. He broke bread with them, making of it a symbol of his own body, soon to be broken. He drank wine with them, making of it a symbol of his own blood, soon to be shed. Remembering this, his disciples saw in bread a symbol of themselves as his risen body on earth, in wine a symbol of his continuing life in which they shared. In breaking bread and sharing wine, they remembered his witness unto death and the triumph of his spirit. As do we.

[The bread is broken and the wine poured into the common cup.]

In sharing this broken bread we become one body, remembering the man who went about doing good, healing the sick and bringing relief to the oppressed. As we eat of it, may we feel our oneness, remembering all who have striven to restore our broken humanity. May we share the Spirit with which Jesus was anointed.

[The bread is shared.] (continued overleaf)

In sharing this wine, we affirm that we are of one blood with all who share the human form. As we drink of the one cup, may we drink of the one Spirit, remembering all whose love and wisdom have blessed the world. May we share the Spirit that God pours out on his sons and daughters.

[The wine is shared. Then silence for personal prayer and reflection.]

May the Spirit that was in Jesus,
the Spirit that roared and blazed into his disciples,
the Spirit that makes one body of all
who love and serve the Lord,
be with us and among us, now and always.

Amen. Go in peace.

POPPY FIELD IN SUMMER
Ofton, Suffolk – June

Bright summer poppies,
field of red, breathtaking
beneath the cloudless blue,
the blazing sun.

Bright June poppies
flaming in the green
Suffolk lushness
to fill the soul with joy.

These are not
November poppies,

the brave, sad poppies
of remembrance;

but those too once
blazed red beneath
a summer sky, on bloody fields
where soldiers die.

SUMMER SKY
Fynn Valley, Suffolk – July

Standing beneath
a blue summer sky
with larks rising
in exultation and
poppies nodding red
amid the ripening corn –
could there be more
than this to live for?
Would not this moment
suffice for all eternity?

SUN OF RIGHTEOUSNESS
'...the sun of righteousness will rise with healing in its wings.'
(Malachi 4: 2)

The fiery power of heaven
rises in glory to its zenith,
drenching our northern lands
with warmth and light;

(continued overleaf)

bidding the waving grass to grow,
the butterflies to flutter by,
the scarlet-studded fields to ripen
and yield their harvest bounty.

With joy in our hearts we greet
the summer sun that gives us life,
and we hail the sun of righteousness
who shows us how to live it.

FOR LAMMAS
With thanks to Henry David Thoreau

We kindle this flame
to remind us of sunlight falling
without distinction on our fields
and forests, bringing their harvest
to fruition. So are we attached to
the earth and given strength to live,
to love, and to give thanks.

LAMMAS: THERE IS A HARVEST

There is a harvest of the land.
We gather to give thanks for the food
which sustains our bodies.

There is a harvest of the spirit.
We gather to give thanks for the apostles
of truth, and love, and liberty.

The first-fruits of the land's harvest
bring hope of nourishment;
dispel the fear of hunger.
The first-fruits of the spirit's harvest
bring hope of a better world
for all humanity.

Let us give thanks and worship.

FIRST FRUITS: INVOCATION AND BENEDICTION FOR LAMMAS
Deuteronomy 26: 2, 4, 10–11

In our hearts,
if not in our hands,
we bring to this holy place
the first-fruits of the harvest.
In gratitude and worship
we set them before the Creator.
Let us rejoice in all the good things
that God has given us.

In our hearts, if not in our hands,
we brought to this holy place
the first-fruits of the harvest.
In gratitude and worship
we have set them before the Creator
and we have shared them with each other.

Now, as we part, may we be blessed
in all the good things that God has given us.

SEPTEMBER

September – a subtle shift –
autumn creeps softly upon us.
The Earth tilts us towards darkness,
while her bounty still surrounds us.
We give thanks for the circling year
and take its lessons to our hearts.

EARLY AUTUMN PRAYER
Fynn Valley, Suffolk – September

House-martins swoop and swerve
in the bright autumnal sky,
feeding up for the long journey south.
O God of Nature's wonder,
bring them safely back to us in Spring
and grant us all another year of life and plenty.

THIS PRESENT PARADISE
Harvest Festival

We come together in thanksgiving
for this present paradise that is the earth.
We offer bread and wine, flowers and fruit,
to celebrate the goodness of God who has given them.
We read the Divine names
in the fruits of the earth,
and pray that God will read the homage
of love and gratitude in our hearts.

ON THE THIRD DAY – A ROLL CALL OF THE FRUITS OF THE EARTH

'And the earth brought forth grass, and herb yielding seed after
its kind, and the tree yielding fruit, whose seed was in itself, after
his kind: and God saw that it was good. And the evening and the
morning were the third day.'

(Genesis I: 12–13)

Bring Apples to the Harvest Table, and Apricots;
and, with a whiff of salt-fish on a tropical breeze,
bring Ackees and Almonds.

Bring Bananas and Breadfruit, Blackberries and Blueberries,
Barley and Black-eyed peas –
and, from the shrinking rainforest, bring Brazils.

Let there be Cabbage on the harvest table,
and Currants – red, white, and black;
Chestnuts for an autumn fireside, Cranberries, Carrots,
Cauliflowers and Cashews. And Conkers,
for their beauty and their memories.

Bring Dill, Dates, and Damsons; Elderflower cordial and
Elderflower wine; Figs, and long-forgotten Fat-hen and Feverfew.

Bring Ginger and Gooseberries, Grapes and Grapefruit,
Gherkins and Gunga-peas.

Find a place for Hazelnuts; for Hops and Hips and Haws; for
I-tal Illalu and Iceberg lettuce; Jackfruit and Juniper.

(continued overleaf)

Bring Kiwi fruit and Kale; Lemons, Limes, and luscious Lychees.

With thanksgiving, bring Marrows and Melons, Maize, Mint and Mushrooms; even Nettles, neglected and reviled but good for us and for butterflies.

Oranges and Olives, Onions and Oats, all have their place; and Plums and Plantains, Pears and Peaches, Peppers and Parsley, Potatoes and Pistachios.

Bring Quince. Bring Raspberries and Rice, Rosemary – for remembrance – and Runner beans.

Put Strawberries on the Table, and Starfruit; Spinach (to make us strong!), Soya and Sugar – both beet and cane.

Bring Turnips and Tangerines; Thyme, and even Truffles (if you can find them!).

Bring Ugly fruit; holy Vervain and fragrant Valerian; Walnuts, Wheat, and Watercress.

Xeranthemum, for eternity, takes its place at the table, and, for mortality, autumn leaves, golden with Xanthophyll.

Bring Yams – and Zinnias, to represent the flowers!

Let us give thanks for this Harvest Table, groaning but far from complete, and all that God found good on the Third Day.

OTHER HARVESTS

There are other harvests from other Days of Creation than the Third: hard-won harvests of the sea and the earth's deep places, too often squandered and misused.

Whether we eat meat or just eat what we grow on felled forests, drained wetlands, and ploughed prairies, none of us can stand aside and say we have no part in this.

In humility, then, in sorrow mixed with joy, we give thanks for all that we take from this good earth, and we ask for wisdom to use it justly and with compassion.

May it be so.

FOR THE HARVEST

For the harvest of the year, hard-won from an earth at once bountiful and grudging, we give thanks.

For all our cleverness, all our technology, all our pride in our own achievements, we are as dependent on our mother-planet as were our forebears, remote in time, who first scratched a living from its surface.

We are sojourners here. With reverence and wisdom we must till the soil. It is not ours to own and dispose of as we will. 'The earth is the Lord's and the fullness thereof.' And it is our children's and our children's children's too.

(continued overleaf)

For them it must be as fertile, as green, and as rich in life as it has been for us. We must do what we can to make it so, as faithful stewards of this good earth. For the harvest of the year, we give thanks...

And for the harvest of the years we give thanks: the harvest of shared faith and shared work, a shared spirit and a shared endeavour. As the harvest of the earth is both an ending and a beginning, so may the harvest of the years, the harvest of faithful, hopeful, loving community – for all its endless endings – be always rich with new beginnings.

May it be so.

AS LEAVES FLAME

As leaves flame yellow, red, and gold,
then fall,
and flames and sweet aromas
rise from autumn bonfires,
so too we kindle our chalice-flame
in thanks for the season's beauty
and the love that makes us one.

SEASON OF SPIDERS
'The spider taketh hold with her hands, and is in kings' palaces.'
(Proverbs 30: 28)

*'The pattern of those who take to patrons other than God is like
the spider who builds a nest: for the flimsiest of houses is surely the
spider's nest.'*
(The Qur'an 29: 41)

It is the season of spiders –
   octopedal October spinners,
   menacing creators,
   plump, well-fed destroyers,
whose intricate, artful engineering
is strung improbably around our houses
and across our gardens,
glistening in autumn sunshine:
   perilous, beautiful, fatal traps
   for many an unwary, drunken
   end-of-season wasp.

THE FOREST OF ENGLAND: AN AUTUMNAL MEDITATION

*'Look at the animals roaming the forest: God's spirit dwells within
them... Look too at the great trees of the forest: God's spirit is
present in all plants as well.'* – (Pelagius, letter to a friend)

*'Take your busy heart to the art museum and the
chamber of commerce
but take it also to the forest.'*
(Mary Oliver, 'What Can I Say')

In the damp autumn woods,
beautiful and still,
lives the memory of the Wildwood,
the great forest of England.

A squirrel, so it's said,
could travel through the land
from end to end
and never touch the ground.

We think it's gone, but the forest
is still there, waiting to reclaim
the dark earth, laid down in the
leaves of countless autumns.

It waits – to connect the scattered
woods and spinneys, the hedgerows
and the field oaks; spreading out from
Sherwood's remnants and from Epping's.

Even in the city it is waiting,
quietly masquerading as tree-lined
streets and leafy squares, as parks and
shaded gardens and places of the dead.

Before axes of stone and bronze and iron
the Wildwood fell, but the great forest of
England is still there – you can see it waiting,
waiting for us to go.

THE LAST AUTUMN
For the Ash Trees

Autumn,
sweetest of seasons
and the saddest,
though filled with promise.

Yet for every tree
an autumn will come
when the leaves fall
for the last time,

As there will be
for each of us.

ALL HALLOWS' EVE

At this time when frivolity makes light of ghosts and witches
and wandering spirits, we take time out to remember the
victims of superstition and unreason, and their real suffering.

In sorrow and repentance, we pray for all 'that died unbaptised,
or excommunicate, or laid violent hands upon themselves', and
were denied burial in hallowed ground and the refuge of your
peace, by misguided piety.

We pray that their spirits find rest, though we know that your
love has always been broader than our narrow hypocrisies.

(continued overleaf)

We pray for all branded 'witch' – suffering torture and death because of malice and fearful ignorance, not only in the past but in our world today.

And we pray for the children tortured and murdered because there are still people who, in their evil delusion, suppose themselves to be magicians or exorcists, manipulators – with blood and sacrifice – of 'spirits' and 'supernatural powers'.

We give thanks for the gifts of reason and science that dispel the darkness of ignorance and superstition, pledging ourselves to carry their light in our minds and hearts for the sake of humanity.

WITNESSES: FOR ALL SOULS' DAY

'...we also are compassed about with so great a cloud of witnesses...'
(Hebrews 12: 1)

On this All Souls' Day, when thanks are given for the faithful
of the ages, we recall with gratitude all who have worshipped
here and been this congregation through the centuries. In
their time they maintained the witness that we, in our time,
must now maintain.

May they rest in peace, O God, and as they walked humbly
with you in loving fellowship, so too may we.

Amen.

LEGACY: FOR ALL SOULS'

In Memoriam – Vera W. H. Reed

This is the year's quiet time, poised between the fading
memories of a summer that has gone and the prospect of
darker days and longer nights, of a bright festival to relieve
the gloom, and then the long, cold haul to re-awakening and
rebirth.

We give thanks for the circling year and its changing seasons,
because we need them all.

And we give thanks for those who, as we do now, watched the
passing seasons before passing into the Great Mystery in their
turn – leaving us the legacy of their busy lives.

LATE POPPY
Fynn Valley, Suffolk – November

A single poppy,
bright spot of red
amid November's
mud and gloom:
even Nature
harbours memories
of Flanders field
and wears her token
of remembrance.

ROCKETS
Recasting of words from a letter by Francis Edward Ledwidge,
killed on the Western Front, 31 July 1917

If you visit the front,
come up the line at night
to watch the German rockets.
They have white crests
which throw a pale flame
across no-man's land:

white bursting into green,
green changing into blue,
blue bursting and dropping down
in purple torrents.

It is like the end of a beautiful world.

NO GREATER LOVE

'Greater love hath no man than this, that a man lay down his life for his friends.'
(John 15: 13)

Together to the war they went, those regiments of 'pals', those home-town friends.

Together at the war they died, or limped back maimed or blind or scarred in body or in mind.

They went to war as patriots, but they fought as friends, as all soldiers do, they say, with comradeship the only bond when bullets fly.

We remember the names of those we never knew, carved on stones that, to the young, are monuments to ancient history – unless, perhaps, they are the names of those who died in bloody follies of more recent date – and war is always folly, just or not.

We may say they died for God and King, or Queen and Country, but, in truth, they died for a greater love: they died for their friends.

May peace eternal be upon them.

REMEMBERING KING EDMUND
Sometime patron saint of England (d. 20 November 869)

' *In this year the host rode across Mercia into East Anglia...and the same winter King Edmund fought against them, and the Danes had the victory, and they slew the king.'* (The Anglo-Saxon Chronicle)

God of the ages,
on this autumn day
we remember a young king
who died for his people and his faith,
and all who have done the same.

Grant us the faith
that strengthened him
in the face of his enemies
and their reckless hate;
the loyalty to you that never wavered.

We ask to share in the virtues
that he learned from Jesus:
humility, charity, kindness to those in need,
and courage in the face of evil:
the will to restrain the oppressor
and protect the weak.

Recalling Edmund, saint and martyr,
free East Anglia's last king, we pray
to be true witnesses for your peace and justice
in this, his ancient realm, and in a world where inhumanity
too often prevails.

Amen.

DISMISSAL FOR SAINT EDMUND'S DAY
(20th November)

God of mercy,
by whose grace your martyrs and witnesses
overcome in spirit the malice of their persecutors,
help us to win the struggle within ourselves.
Empower us to be faithful to your loving Spirit
when our time of testing comes.

Amen.

IN PRAISE OF MUSIC: FOR SAINT CECILIA'S DAY
(22nd November)
*'Praise the Lord with the harp: sing unto him with the psaltery
and an instrument with ten strings. Sing unto him a new song:
play skilfully with a loud noise.'*
(Psalm 33: 2–3)

We give thanks today
for music and musicians;
for songs and singers;
for orchestras and bands of every kind
and for the instruments they play.

We give thanks for composers and conductors,
for choirs and quartets, dances and dancers,
and all the concertos, symphonies, operas,
and musicals that move us, entertain us,
or raise our spirits to the heights.

(continued overleaf)

We give thanks for organs and organists,
hymns and hymn-writers, bells and bell-ringers,
cantors and muezzins – all whose hands and voices
call us to prayer and accompany our worship.

We give thanks for the diversity of genres
in which music is expressed – classical, jazz,
and rock'n'roll; reggae, rap, and all the rest,
everything pleasing somebody,
nothing pleasing everybody.
May we learn to tolerate each other's tastes!

The lives of most of us would be the poorer
without music, so let's give thanks for it
and for the multifarious ways to listen to it.
Let's praise with harp, trumpet, and guitar...
Let's sing new songs, and the old ones too.
Let's play as skilfully as we can,
with as loud a noise as neighbourliness allows!

And may harmony replace discord the world over.

ADVENT ANTICIPATION

Autumn's beauty has been blown away,
winter's darkness enfolds us,
and spring seems a distant prospect;
but your light and hope have not abandoned us,
O God – whom we abandon.

We give our thanks for the great festival
that now approaches,
as we give thanks for him whose birth it celebrates.

May your love in him be bright
before us and within us
in this time of anticipation.

ADVENT: CANDLES AND CHRISTMAS TREES

It is Advent,
and to welcome
the light of the world
we light up the long winter nights
and the gloomy winter days
with candles and with Christmas trees.

Jesus may have seen candles,
but he never saw a Christmas tree,
though if he had, he would have loved it.
He would have loved the joy
its twinkling lights bring to children
and to all child-like hearts.

It is Advent.
O God, bless your forests
and teach us to care for them.
Bless the trees we take to bring
beauty, light, and fragrance to our homes.
And bless all who approach Christmas
with love in their hearts.

PASSING THROUGH: FOR ADVENT

May wisdom and generosity
be ours in this season of anticipation,
passing through its busy days
with love in our hearts,
wonder in our souls,
and light in our minds.

May it be so!

ADVENT CANDLES
For the Ipswich Unitarians, December 2012

May the Advent candles
light your way
to Christmas.

And may the light
of Christmas
shine among you
at the gateway
of the year.

UNITARIANS AND CHRISTMAS – A THANKSGIVING

At Christmas, we give thanks for the birth of Jesus – whenever it actually was!

And we give thanks for all that he said and did for the salvation of the human spirit, which he shared with us.

We give thanks for all the poets, musicians, and mythmakers who, down the centuries, have given us the means with which to deepen our devotions and kindle our imaginations at this sacred time.

And because we stand in the tradition of a liberal faith, we give thanks for what our predecessors have added to the season's treasury.

We think of John Milton and his poem, 'On the Morning of Christ's Nativity', which bids us *'join thy voice unto the Angel Quire'* and greet the infant Lord *'with hallowed fire'.*

We think of Coleridge and his 'Religious Musings' one Christmas Eve, when he wrote: *'I seem to view the vision of the heavenly multitude, who hymned the song of peace o'er Bethlehem's fields!'*

And we think of Charles Dickens – how could we not! – with his 'Christmas Carol' and all those other Christmas Books and Stories; his own re-telling of the Nativity; his declaration that *'There seems a magic in the very name of Christmas.'*

(continued overleaf)

We make our own these words of his: *'Nearer and closer to our hearts be the Christmas spirit, the spirit of active usefulness, perseverance, cheerful discharge of duty, kindness, and forbearance.'*

Dickens writes of *'a merry company of children assembled round that pretty German toy, a Christmas Tree'*. Prince Albert gave England this 'pretty toy', but it's said that a Unitarian minister, Charles Follen, took it to America.

We read to our children Beatrix Potter's little book, 'The Tailor of Gloucester', where *'...all the beasts can talk, in the night between Christmas Eve and Christmas Day in the morning'*, and when *'From all the roofs and gables in the old wooden houses came merry voices singing the old Christmas rhymes.'*

We sing the stirring words of Edmund Hamilton Sears' hymn, 'It Came Upon the Midnight Clear' and Longfellow's great poem, 'I Heard the Bells on Christmas Day', with gratitude for these and for all in our tradition who have added to the seasonal store of hymns and carols in which we delight.

At Christmas we give thanks for the birth of Jesus, our brother. We give thanks for the chance to celebrate this bright festival in the darkness of the year. And we give thanks for everyone who has added to its holiness, its joy, and its glorious light.

THE SAME OLD CAROLS

'Why do we always sing the same old carols?'
someone always asks,
'Why do we never sing the new ones?'
The new ones, that is, which get written,
and forgotten, every year.

We sing the same old carols because,
from somewhere out of sight,
other voices are already singing them,
calling us to sing them too:

'O Come All Ye Faithful',
'The First Nowell', and 'Silent Night';
'Good King Wenceslas', 'Away in a Manger',
' O Little Town of Bethlehem', and all the rest.

Up they well from somewhere deeper
than our own memories, our own past.
As we sing them, we join, not just with each other,
but with our parents and our grandparents,

with their parents and their grandparents,
all singing down the Decembers,
in church and chapel, pub and lamp-lit street;
in front-parlours around pianos
and twinkling Christmas trees.

They sing with us and in us and through us,
spirits of Christmases past, benign and loving,
blessing this holy time, as ours will bless

(continued overleaf)

the Christmases to come, singing in voices
that the Earth has yet to hear.

We sing the same old carols because,
though dry reason and dull fact deny it,
the angels and the shepherds sang them
on that holy night when Christ was born.

MY BETHLEHEM

I went to Bethlehem once –
    in a taxi from Jerusalem
    along a guarded road.

It wasn't Christmas,
    or Christmassy.

I found an undistinguished town
    with little but its name to sing about.
    And a church.

An ancient church with a low door,
    to keep the crusaders from riding
    their horses in – or so it's said.

Within, Byzantine gloom –

and a queue for the grotto where, or so
    some canny priest once told an empress,
    Christ was born.

I didn't join it.

The taxi headed back to Jerusalem,
 through checkpoints where a wall now stands.
 I looked back on a rock-strewn hillside.

A few sheep grazed
 above the troubled little town.
 And I saw my Bethlehem.

THANKSGIVING AT CHRISTMAS

God of our hearts, who comes to us
in the wisdom of the ancients
and in the innocence of a new-born child,
we come to you in thanksgiving
on this Christmas Day.

We thank you for Jesus:
for the Way of love that he showed us,
and walked himself.

We thank you for the stories of his birth,
that charm us as children
and impart deeper lessons when we grow up.

We thank you for all the joy
and generosity of Christmas-time;
for its good fellowship and its good food –
if we are fortunate enough to have some.

(continued overleaf)

We thank you for the season's myth and magic,
antidotes to our world-weariness and cynicism.
But remind us of our duty to those who suffer
and grieve on this Christmas Day.

God of our inmost hearts
and of the starry heavens above,
make of us your loving children,
true sisters and brothers of Jesus,
and members of that new humanity
of which he was the firstborn.

So may we enter your Kingdom
and be messengers of your peace.

Amen.

TESTIMONY

'We meet on holy ground,
Brought into being as life encounters life,
As personal histories merge into the communal story...'

(Richard S. Gilbert: *In the Holy Quiet of this Hour*)

ON BEING A UNITARIAN

I am a Unitarian.

For me, that means believing in God as Divine Unity, and in the Oneness of Humanity and all Creation. It means believing in Jesus the man: the human teacher and revealer of the Way to live in this world. It means believing that the real church is the community of those who share his spirit and have become its new body. It means knowing that the Divine Way is also known to great souls in traditions other than my own.

And I am a Unitarian because of the spirit and the values that I seek to express: love of neighbour, kindness, and mutual respect; an open mind and an open heart; constructive tolerance of the beliefs that are dear to other people of goodwill, whether as individuals or faith communities.

I feel myself to be in fellowship with all who share my beliefs and hold them in the same spirit to which I aspire. And I share fellowship with people who have different beliefs but the same spirit.

But fellowship is hard with people who are intolerant and disrespectful of my beliefs, or who despise the honest, peaceful, humble faith of anyone, whether in my tradition or any other.

FIRST MEMORIES OF CHURCH
Claremont Free Church (Baptist), London NW2 (1947–1956)

'Suffer little children, and forbid them not to come unto me: for of such is the kingdom of God.'
(Matthew 19: 14)

Watching sunbeams in Sunday School.

The Harvest Festival's fruity, fragrant mountain,
clustered round the sheaf-shaped loaf.
And singing about ploughing and scattering – in NW2!

The baptistery, mysterious beneath the floor,
where white-clad grown-ups were sometimes
wrestled to immersion. And wishing it could be
a swimming-pool on summer days!

The solemn service on Remembrance Day,
with a radio in church – to listen to the silence.
On every breast, a poppy.

Excitement as the Christmas bazaar heralded the magic.
And singing carols by candlelight, then walking home
beneath the stars with mum and dad.

The stories of Jesus and the community's love
that made them real.

THE ANTI-CIVILIZATION LEAGUE

'I think of the old ACL from time to time. We were very avant-garde, weren't we? Who said there is something wrong with a young man who is not a radical and something wrong with a mature man who is?'

(Andrew S. Reed)

When I was nine, or thereabouts, and he was ten, my brother and I, and his mate, Michael, from up the road, founded the Anti-Civilization League. We were its only members.

We were 'deep greens' before that term was coined. We were pledged to roll back the engulfing tide of brick and concrete that threatened the green earth and its wild things – even though the nearest wood to us was Cricklewood!

We were non-violent (I like to think!), but direct action was allowed, even if no one else got the point. We were in solidarity with the earth's indigenous peoples – always 'Indians' and never 'Cowboys'.

That was all a lifetime ago. But something of the Anti-Civilization League is alive in me still. After all, that consuming, destroying tide sweeps over the green earth still, and with mounting power – blanketing the meadows with asphalt, brick, and concrete; felling the forests; killing the seas; wrenching ever more of Darwin's 'endless forms most beautiful and most wonderful' from Life's fraying and tattered web.

In 1950s London three little boys took their stand, and maybe in the annals of those who would save the Earth from humanity, and humanity from itself, the Anti-Civilization League deserves a mention!

THANK YOU, AMERICA

I want to say 'thank you' to America
for three of her daughters:

for Mary Oliver and her poetry,
for Emmylou Harris and her songs,
for Barbara Kingsolver and her novels.

In them the true spirit of America lives,
as once it lived in Whitman, Thoreau,
and Emily Dickinson

For them all, America,
I say thank you.

HAPPY BIRTHDAY, MUM!
For Vera W. H. Reed – 26 October 2012

' Happy Birthday, Mum!'

How many millions will say those words today, or any day, and
have the greeting met with smiles and kisses,
a mother's tears of joy and her warm embrace?

But there comes a time when the tears are ours; when we say
those words to a memory; in sad remembrance of someone
we love as much as ever, but who isn't here to smile at our
greeting; to kiss us and enfold us with her loving presence, as
once, as always, she did.

(continued overleaf)

My mother died thirty-nine years ago, and I still miss her,
though you may not know it, and, mostly, it might not show.
But today is her birthday, so: 'Happy Birthday, Mum!'

JUST SO YOU KNOW...

Just so you know...
I believe that the world is round, that Elvis is dead,
and that smoking causes cancer.
I believe that Darwin was right,
and that his theory of evolution is essentially true.
I believe that the Holocaust really happened,
and that those who deny it are those most likely to repeat it.
I believe that the attacks of 9/11 were entirely and solely the
work of al-Qaeda's pseudo-Islamic terrorists.
I believe that global warming is really happening
and that human activity has a very great deal to do with it.
I believe that Shakespeare wrote most, if not all, of the plays
and poems attributed to him.
I believe that the Turin Shroud is a medieval fake.
I believe that Neil Armstrong walked on the Moon.
And I believe that, although there probably is intelligent life
somewhere else in the universe, it is too far away for us to find
it – or it us.

I believe that Jesus really lived and died in Palestine, and that
the four gospels – five, if you include Thomas – preserve a
good deal of what he taught.
I believe that reason, critical thought, and the scientific method
are indispensable aids in the search for truth.
And I believe that the purveyors of superstition,
junk science, conspiracy theories, fundamentalism,

and other mumbo-jumbo get far more attention
than they deserve, which, mostly, is none.

CREDO

I believe in God, the Divine Unity,
origin and sustaining power of the universe.

I believe that the man, Jesus of Nazareth,
was our brother; that he knew God as Father,
lived and died in Palestine,
and walked the Way of love for us to follow.

I believe in the Holy Spirit, the Breath of God,
through which we are given life itself, and the inspiration to
love our neighbours as ourselves.

I believe that truth and wisdom have been found
and revealed by many great souls, prophets,
and messengers of the Divine.

I believe that the Divine is also revealed
in the courage, compassion, and simple kindness
of countless men and women.

I believe that humanity is One,
that all life is One,
that all of nature is One:
a Divine Unity.

INDEX

ABOUT THE AUTHOR

Clifford Martin Reed was born in 1947 in London. His father, Lionel Reed, was then a Baptist minister. Lionel's own spiritual path led him into the Unitarian ministry when Cliff was a boy. Cliff's personal commitment to the Unitarian movement began in his teens. He became active in the Unitarian Young People's League and was its National President at the age of 20. He went to Guyana with Voluntary Service Overseas as a librarian – his first profession. Returning to the United Kingdom, he worked at Dr Williams's Library in London, and became a member of Golders Green Unitarian Church.

Called to ministry, he trained at Unitarian College, Manchester, and studied theology at Manchester University. In 1976 he began his 36-year ministry at Ipswich, along with service to two rural congregations in Suffolk. In 1992 he undertook an exchange ministry in Bloomington, Illinois. Always active in the wider Unitarian movement, he has served as Secretary of the International Council of Unitarians & Universalists, and as President of the General Assembly of Unitarian & Free Christian Churches. He retired from ministry in 2012.

He began writing devotional material as a student, contributing to several anthologies and three hymnals. His publications include *We Are Here* (Lindsey Press, 1992), *The Way of the Pilgrim* (Ipswich Unitarians, 1993), *Celebrating the Flame* (Van der Heijden Publishing, 1997), *Spirit of Time and Place* (Lindsey Press, 2002), *Sacred Earth* (Lindsey Press, 2010), *'Till The Peoples All Are One': Darwin's Unitarian Connections* (Lindsey Press, 2011), and *Unitarian? What's That?* (Lindsey Press, 1999, 2011).

Lightning Source UK Ltd.
Milton Keynes UK
UKOW02f1806310515

252646UK00001B/15/P